# FREMANTLE

# BEYOND THE ROUND HOUSE

**DAVID WEBB & DAVID WARREN**

LONGLEY BOOKS
Fremantle

*Fremantle* **BEYOND THE ROUND HOUSE**
Copyright © 2005 by David Webb, David Warren and Longley
Books


Published by: Longley Books
22 Walker Street, South Fremantle, Western Australia 6162
Email: jenijone@iinet.net.au
Fax: 61 8 9430 4418

Design: Caris Wilkinson
Cover photo: David Webb

Printed by: WIP Print Pty Ltd
18 Southport Street, West Leederville, Western Australia 6008

ISBN: 0-646-44568-5

# ABOUT THE AUTHORS

David Webb and David Warren are former metropolitan newspaper executives with extensive experience in all facets of journalism, including feature writing and editing. They have developed a special interest in researching and writing local histories, recording the events, the people involved and the matters of significance or interest that occurred. This is their first co-authored book, written in conjunction with John Longley who initiated the idea and oversaw the project.

John Longley AM is one of Australia's most outstanding international yachtsmen. Among a notable record of achievements, he was project manager and a crew member of *Australia II's* historic America's Cup win at Newport in 1983, general manager of the Cup's defence at Fremantle in 1987 and chief executive of the HM Bark Endeavour Foundation. Among his many awards he was made a member of the Order of Australia (AM) in 1984 for his services to yachting and, a decade later, was named Fremantle Citizen of the Year. A family man and long-term resident of Fremantle, he continues to have a major role in the Port City's affairs as chief executive of the Fremantle Chamber of Commerce. He also maintains his active sporting interests as a keen cyclist and sailor.

# FOREWORD

Walking around the Port City of Fremantle I often see visitors looking curiously and somewhat bemused at the cityscape before them. I usually resist the impulse to introduce myself and offer what I know about the special place that I have called home since the mid-1970s. So much history - so many stories - where would you start? And yet for visitors, their time in Fremantle is surely diminished unless they at least know some of the stories - hence this book.

*Fremantle* **BEYOND THE ROUND HOUSE** is not meant to be a comprehensive history of Fremantle. Rather, it is a collection of 50 of the countless stories that could be written on this unique place. The common thread is that each story starts with something that still exists, that visitors can stand before, enter into, or reach out and touch. From the actual object we look at the people behind each place and their unique contribution to the ongoing saga of Fremantle.

People who know Fremantle well may wonder why I have chosen these stories and not others. It is simply a personal choice of stories that I find interesting and enjoy telling. Not surprisingly as the book developed I realised how much more there was to learn even about the stories I thought I knew well. I suspect that people who have lived in Fremantle all their lives will also find that there is much here that will be new to them. David Webb and David Warren have done a wonderful job in ferreting out these stories.

I hope you enjoy *Fremantle* **BEYOND THE ROUND HOUSE**. I know that after you have walked or ridden around Fremantle, found the places that we talk about and then read the stories, you will have a much better idea why Fremantle is so special and indeed so loved by its people.

John Longley
Fremantle 2005

# CONTENTS

**THE FREMANTLE TRAIL MAP**
**INSIDE BACK COVER**

# Why the Round House has a poetic touch

The Round House
10 Arthur Head
Map Ref: 1

**T**he **Round House is well recognised** as Western Australia's oldest surviving building. What makes it even more interesting is the background story of the man who designed it.

Henry Willey Reveley, the colony's first appointed civil engineer, had been a close friend of the English poet Percy Bysshe Shelley, at one time saving his life from drowning in a boating accident in Italy.

That incident occurred eight years before Reveley and his beautiful wife Amelia arrived at Fremantle in mid-1829, when the building of a prison was an important priority for the small colony. Tenderers selected the prominent site at Arthur's Head as the most suitable to meet the associated problems of sudden influxes in population coupled with a lively seamen's environment.

Reveley's radial design for the prison was unconventional, most likely influenced by that of a much larger gaol designed some 40 years earlier by his architect father. Built from the limestone quarried nearby, the 12-sided building comprised a gaoler's residence and eight cells opening onto a central courtyard (where stocks were later installed).

The gaol's construction took just six months to complete from August 1830, a remarkable achievement. But Reveley's unusual flat roof design, an idea he possibly copied from a building in Cape Town where he had worked as the civil engineer before coming to WA, caused headaches. The roof leaked, and continued to do so despite renovations and constant attention over the next few years. Reveley blamed poor workmanship for the problem, not the design or the porous materials used - including the limestone - which encouraged water to move in on those inside wishing to move out.

Other buildings were progressively added to what became an Arthur's Head complex. These included a courthouse in 1837 and two lighthouses and cottages to house harbour-masters and harbour personnel.

After the new Fremantle Prison was built in the mid-1850s, the Round House role changed from a gaol for short-term offenders, to a police lock-up and, in 1900, to living quarters for a constable and his family. This was when a time ball erected on the seaward side near the lighthouse became a new feature, its purpose to give mariners a precise daily time to check their chronometers for accurate navigation. Hoisted to the top of a tower three minutes before 1pm, the ball was released precisely on the hour, activated by an electrical signal from the Perth Astronomical Observatory which, in turn, triggered a shot from a cannon.

Reveley's other most noted enterprise in Fremantle was the design of the Whalers Tunnel beneath the Round House. From 1831 until he returned to England in 1838, his work mostly centred on Perth projects such as the building of a courthouse, a water mill, an official residence for the Governor and the construction of what is now known as the Causeway across the Swan River.

HENRY REVELEY'S friendship with Shelley and his wife Mary in Italy came about through a family introduction and a common interest in boating (young Henry had moved to Italy with his mother and stepfather where he was brought up after his father had died). Reveley also designed and built a boat for the poet. The family connection is mentioned in various published letters by the poet, including the reference (right) to the incident in April 1821, when Shelley, who could not swim, was helped ashore by Reveley after their boat capsized on an inland waterway. Some 15 months later, the poet drowned during a gale in the Mediterranean.

By then Reveley had returned to England, where he began working as a designer/ engineer and met his future wife Amelia. Eight years on, the first stones of the Round House were laid.

'My Dear Henry.

*Our ducking last night has added fire, instead of quenching the nautical ardour which produced it; and I consider it a good omen in any enterprise, that it begins in evil; as being more probable that it will end in good. I hope you have not suffered from it. I am rather feverish, but very well as to the side, whence I expected the worst consequences. I send you directions for the complete equipment of our boat, since you have so kindly promised to undertake it. In putting into execution, a little more or less expense in so trifling an affair, is to be disregarded. I need not say that the approaching season invites expedition. You can put her in hand immediately, and write the day on which we may come for her. All good be with you. We expect with impatience the arrival of our false friends, who have so long cheated us with delay; and Mary unites with me in desiring, that, as you participated equally in the crime, you should not be omitted in the expiation.*

*Adieu. Yours faithfully, S.'*

Excerpt from Shelley's letter to Henry Reveley after their river mishap. Dated Pisa, 17th April, 1821

**Percy Bysshe Shelley**

# Tunnel opened way for a whaling industry

Whalers Tunnel
Arthur Head, High Street
Map Ref: 1

**T**he day after the first whale was harpooned in Cockburn Sound there was great excitement in Fremantle. Guns were fired for several hours during the morning to mark what was considered a significant and memorable event.

It was on Friday, June 9, 1837, that the whale was spotted and, subsequently, chased, killed and hauled to the jetty at Bathers Bay. Just eight years earlier, Captain Charles Howe Fremantle had stepped ashore on the same beach to proclaim the land as British territory.

Today, the only remaining visible evidence of those early activities is the much-restored Whalers Tunnel, carved through the limestone cliff beneath the Round House. As with the building above it, the 100-metre short-cut from Bathers Beach to central Fremantle was the creation of the colony's civil engineer, Henry Reveley. It was built specifically by the Fremantle Whaling Company, founded by John Bateman, to provide direct access for transporting processed whale products from the shore-based whalers' station to the town. The tunnel took five months to complete and was ready for use by January 1838.

*Bathers Beach, where whales were once dragged ashore.*

Historical records show that bay-whaling from a fixed shore base was a comparatively low-capital industry, requiring 'the provision of four to six boats, try-pots for boiling down the catch, rough huts for cooperage and boiling, and the payment of wages, partly in the form of provisions and rum, for sixteen to twenty men.' Because of the somewhat low-key nature of the operation, the whalers were restricted to the shallower waters of Bathers Bay, their main catch being the slower right-whale, less valued for its oil than its bone. Whale bone was then used in the manufacture of umbrellas and various millinery, such as women's corsets.

Not surprisingly, the early days of whaling were not without hazard. On August 7, 1837, a man was killed while trying to harpoon a whale. People on shore had a clear view of the incident, describing how John Stevens was killed by a blow from the fluke of one of the giant mammals. A month earlier, six young men had disappeared in their whaleboat, presumed drowned. They had set out to search for a company boat which had broken its moorings and was last seen drifting northwards from Carnac Island. However, time lapsed and the men did not return. Later, the empty whaleboat and the other boat, along with some wreckage and a man's cap, were found washed up on the beach north of Fremantle.

Initially, the whaling was a joint venture between the Fremantle company and a Perth group, Northern Fisheries, which operated from nearby Carnac Island. They had a promising start with the total export of 71 tonnes of oil and four-and-a-half tonnes of bone, earning more than the export revenue for wool. However, the partnership ended in 1838 when Northern Finance closed because of various inefficiencies and costs. The Fremantle company also had to shut down in 1840 when the demand for whale oil and bone declined rapidly, but was able to reopen three years later with a revival in world market prices. As an industry, some 15 whaling stations were to operate eventually around the WA coastline.

*The tunnel in 1901.*

After the Fremantle Whaling Company closed its operations in 1850, the Whalers Tunnel continued to be used variously for access purposes, whether for people or for carrying electric cables or water pipes. In the early 1900s, a spur tunnel was linked to the back of the quarters of the newly built Fort Arthur Head, supposedly an escape route for military personnel under attack.

However, by 1930 the tunnel was in such poor repair it had been barricaded at both ends with galvanized iron, to be replaced by gates several years later. From then until comparatively recently the tunnel was closed on and off because of continuing safety concerns, its future always hanging in the balance. Some repairs were attempted but were not satisfactory.

Its final restoration came with a joint project between the State Government and the City of Fremantle which brought about permanent public access in June 2001.

# Jetty's remains a reminder of early port

Bathers Bay
Map Ref: 1

**W**orld renowned ceramic sculptor Joan Campbell - once described as a national cultural treasure - was an enthusiastic champion of Bathers Bay and its connection to the earliest history of the Swan River Colony.

Mrs Campbell, who had her workshop at the beach, once wrote that she drew inspiration from waves pounding on the shore of the bay. Flotsam and jetsam gathered from the bay was often incorporated in her work. But her commitment to the area and its history extended beyond her work. In the mid-1990s she was responsible for the construction of the Long Jetty replica and other timber artwork on the beach. The Long Jetty had made the bay the Colony's principal port area in the 19th century, before the construction of Fremantle Harbour, and the remains of the jetty piles can still be seen in the ocean, particularly at low tide.

*Picture, Frances Andrijich*

*Joan Campbell at work in her Bathers Bay workshop in 1995.*

More than 40 years before the construction of the jetty, the bay played a major role in the beginning of European settlement in WA. The beach lies immediately south of Arthur Head, where on May 2, 1829 Captain Charles Howe Fremantle made his first landing on the mainland to take formal possession of the west coast of New Holland on behalf of Great Britain. The beach is now also generally acknowledged as the site of the mainland proclamation of the Colony by Captain Frederick Irwin just over six weeks later.

The first European camp was established close in the lee of Arthur Head by Fremantle, later Admiral Sir Charles Fremantle and the son of Admiral Sir Thomas Fremantle, a British hero of the Battle of Trafalgar in 1805. When colonists began to arrive later that year the area behind the beach became home to tents and makeshift shelters and later a shanty town. The headland was chosen for the colony's first permanent building, the Round House, in 1830.

A whaling industry began in 1836 and the following year the Fremantle Whaling Company built a stone and wood breakwater jetty, the first in the Colony, in the bay. About 25 metres long and wide enough for a coach with six horses to turn, it survived until about 1870. The company also built a warehouse, a boatshed and several trypots - large pots used for boiling whale blubber into oil - and casks in the bay. The area later became a boat-building centre with the Mews boatshed, built in the 1860s and demolished 80 years later, a landmark. Thomas William Mews, who arrived on *Rockingham* in 1830, built the Swan River's first steamer, *Speculator*. The family of shipwrights built a variety of vessels over many years, including ferries, schooners, lighters and pearling luggers.

*Bathers Bay 1896.*

Another jetty, the 147.5m South Jetty, was built in the 1850s between Bathers Bay and South Bay and was used mainly by lighters which loaded and unloaded cargo for ships at anchor. The need for a more substantial structure to cater for the increasing shipping trade led to the construction of the Long Jetty, also known as the Ocean Jetty, in three stages - in 1873, 1887 and 1896 - to a width of 12.8m and a length of 1.004 kilometres.

The jetty was the gateway for thousands of fortune-seekers bound for the Kalgoorlie goldfields in the 1890s and the economic pipeline for WA in the second half of the 19th century. However, exposed to the ocean and the elements it was not popular with many ships' captains. Vessels at berth were frequently damaged. Captains often complained about difficult conditions and once Fremantle Harbour was constructed the jetty's usefulness to shipping fell dramatically. By 1900 it was all but abandoned. However, serviced by trams and trains, it still had local appeal and demolition was averted by its conversion into a promenade. In 1907 swimming baths were built at its base and an entertainment hall constructed at the end. But this venture was unsuccessful. With insufficient funds for upkeep and exposed to the elements the jetty fell into disrepair. It was demolished in 1921 and the piles - apart from one which was left to demonstrate the original height of the jetty - cut to sea level (picture above right).

Joan Campbell's replica jetty project - part of a project to document the area's history and at the same time provide an artistic recreational environment for visitors - was not without its critics. An adjacent food outlet complained that the structure blocked the ocean views that attracted its patrons and others said it was too high. However, the Fremantle City Council supported the project and it went ahead, funded largely by Mrs Campbell.

Her connection with Bathers Bay had begun in 1975 when she leased the former Kerosene or Dangerous Goods Store as a workshop, saving it from demolition. The store, built in 1884 on land reclaimed from the sea, allowed dangerous goods such as kerosene, which was used for domestic and street lighting, to be stored away from the main settlement. The building was taken over by the Harbour and Lights Department and used for various purposes until the early 1970s when it was earmarked for demolition. Extensive renovation work was carried out in 1987 and it remains a centre for the arts with a significant place in the history and culture of Fremantle.

Mrs Campbell was awarded the MBE in 1978 and the prestigious Ros Bower Fellowship in 1986 for her contribution to the arts. Eleven days before her death in March 1997 the Visual Arts/Crafts Fund of the Australia Council awarded her the Emeritus Medal. Later that year she was awarded a posthumous WA Citizen of the Year award for arts and culture.

# US President's journey to the White House, via Fremantle

Strelitz Buildings
30 Mouat Street
Map Ref: 3

*Herbert Hoover, 1928*

*A group outside the Strelitz Buildings possibly around the time of Herbert Hoover's presence in Fremantle.*

**W** **hen the ambitious and brilliant** American mining engineer Herbert Hoover first visited Fremantle at the age of 28, both he and the port had big futures ahead of them.

That visit, in 1902 with his wife Lou, on his way to Western Australia's eastern goldfields, was the first of his four recorded visits to Fremantle. Hoover, later to become the 31st President of the USA, established an office and workshop in the Strelitz Buildings for Bewick, Moreing and Co. It is even suggested he used an upstairs room as a temporary bedroom.

The building also served as the focal point of a centralised clearing house for supplies and equipment for the company's WA operations. This move by Hoover, an early and ruthless proponent of rationalisation and efficiency in business, did little to endear him to local traders in the goldfields who had previously catered for the company's needs.

Hoover's link with WA, particularly Fremantle, is not widely known. Hoover, born into a Quaker family in Iowa in 1874, had graduated from Stanford University, California, in 1895 in geology and engineering. In 1896 Bewick, Moreing and Co, a British firm with extensive gold-mining interests in WA, asked San Francisco mining expert Louis Janin, to recommend for its WA staff an American engineer who could undertake mining examination and exploration work in the outback. There was one condition: the person had to be 35 years old. The problem was that the person Janin considered suitable - Hoover - was only 22.

But Janin recommended him anyway and Hoover grew a moustache and beard to give him a more mature appearance. Hoover told his San Francisco lawyer to be careful handling his life insurance premiums because he was going to "a very bad country." Many of Bewick, Moreing's engineers in Australia had contracted typhoid fever and six had died of the disease.

Hoover arrived in Albany in May 1897 and headed to Coolgardie to evaluate mines for possible purchase and assess the condition of the company's mines. He wrote: "...Now the boom has broken good engineers are called in as physicians to mend the lame ducks. This is what we do by killing the bad ones immediately. At least that is what I do." He was less than impressed with the calibre of personnel and mining practices in WA, writing to an American friend: "Yankees are not well received. They only have us because they have to. They don't know how to make their mines pay dividends. We do." Gold-mining in WA was undergoing a transition from the speculative excesses of the 'roaring nineties' (1890s) to a new era of scientific, cost-efficient low-grade production and Hoover was at the forefront of the process.

Hoover was not impressed with outback WA generally, describing it as "a country of red dust, black flies and white heat." He wryly remarked to a friend that local chickens were being fed crushed ice to "prevent them from laying hard-boiled eggs." He was described at the time by a journalist as "a slight figure with a pallid complexion, a dull, toneless voice and no sense of humour." Others, however, saw him as amiable and well-informed with the ability to inspire and as a most attentive listener with a phenomenal memory and capacity for work - a "high-pressure man, hard-driving, self-driven Yankee in a hurry."

Hoover recommended that Bewick, Moreing buy the Sons of Gwalia mine, near Leonora, 830 kilometres north-east of Perth. His advice was accepted and in 1898 he took control of the mine which became one of the most efficient and richest gold mines in Australia's history. After 18 months Bewick, Moreing transferred him to their operations in China and by 1902 he had been appointed a director of the company and manager of its WA operations.

By this time Fremantle, with its new port, had replaced Albany as the gateway to WA and it was to be Hoover's entry point each time he arrived to oversee the operation of more than 30 mines and 9000 employees.

He arrived for his first tour of inspection on the P & O liner *China* in early 1902 and spent almost three months in WA. During this time he centralised supply operations, working from the Strelitz Buildings which had been constructed in 1897 as office/warehouse space for German-born merchants and shipping agents, Paul and Richard Strelitz.

The brothers were influential in trade and politics and closely identified with the commercial expansion of Fremantle and Perth during the 1890s gold boom. Paul Strelitz, an inaugural member of the East Fremantle Council, became the Netherlands Consul in WA and Richard was the Consul for Denmark. Their business was strongly connected to the goldmining industry which may explain the link with Hoover's company. They imported explosives, railway and mining machinery. The brothers were also fine arts patrons and the owners of several pleasure launches which were a common sight on the Swan River.

The Strelitzs took advantage of the development of Fremantle as the major trading port to expand their business and despite being interred as aliens during World War I, remained the owner-occupants of the building until 1920. The building has since had several uses - as a paint manufacturing business, a private residence, a restaurant and as business premises. It is now on the National Trust register as a place of historical and/or architectural interest.

Herbert Hoover's last visit to WA was in 1907. He left Bewick, Moreing in 1908 at the age of 34, a successful and wealthy man, to become a mining financier and company director. During and after World War I he gained an international reputation for his direction of huge food relief projects in Europe. He was U.S. Secretary of Commerce under Presidents Harding and Coolidge before gaining the Republican Party nomination and being elected President in 1928. However, his presidency was dogged by the Great Depression and he was defeated by Democrat Franklin D.Roosevelt at the 1932 election. He died in 1964.

# View from the attic brought German Consul's downfall

The Consulate Building
5 Mouat Street
Map Ref: 4

**T**he idiosyncratic three-storey building at the western end of Mouat Street, known as the Consulate, has been through several interesting phases, but perhaps none more interesting than when it was the office of the German Consul.

In earlier days the attic had an excellent view over Fremantle harbour and local tradition has it that the Consul, Carl Peter Ludwig Ratazzi, who was also the Italian Consul, used it to spy on shipping movements in and out of the harbour.

Ratazzi had an interesting background. A relation of an Italian Prime Minister, Urbano Ratazzi, he was born in Frankfurt-on-Main, Germany in 1865 and could trace his origins back to the highly-regarded Italian administrators engaged by the expanding Austrian Empire to administer State affairs. He left Germany in 1889 for Sydney where he went into partnership in an import/export business.

*Carl Ratazzi... an early victim of wartime anti-German hysteria.*

In 1893, after touring overseas on business and marrying in New York, Ratazzi dissolved the partnership and joined the firm of Weber, Lohmann, and Co. He remained with the company until 1900 when he was offered the WA agency for the German shipping company, Norddeutscher-Lloyd Imperial German Mail Steamers. He arrived in Fremantle in October that year and formed a partnership with Otto Lurman, who retired two years later. In 1901 Ratazzi founded the German Club in Fremantle.

Ratazzi was appointed a Justice of the Peace in 1905. Two years later "in recognition of valuable services rendered as Italian Consul" the King of Italy made him a Knight Cross of the Order of the Crown. He was promoted to the higher degree of Knight Officer in 1910. He lived in an elegant two-storey residence, Villa Maria, overlooking the port and had a thriving business.

However, the outbreak of war in 1914 saw this situation change dramatically. The Australian Defence Department took a strong stand against leaders of the German-Australian community. German clubs were closed and Ratazzi and four other German Consuls in Australia were interned. As prominent businessmen their activities were seen as harmful to British-Australian interests. Deposed as Consul for Germany and Italy and his commercial activities suspended, Ratazzi was one of the early victims of the anti-German hysteria of the time. Over-enthusiastic British loyalists smashed the windows of his office and the vessels of the company he represented became prizes of war or holed up in neutral ports. And during a rampage by a 1000-strong group which targeted the business premises and homes of Germans in Fremantle, the Ratazzi residence had every street-facing window broken.

During World War I almost 7,000 Germans were interned. Of these 4,500 were Australian residents before 1914. The rest were sailors from German navy and merchant ships in Australian ports when the war broke out or German citizens living in British territories in South-East Asia and transported to Australia at the request of the British Government.

After the war the Mouat Street building was occupied by various tenants, generally businesses associated with shipping and transport. But it took on a new - and controversial - life in 1971 when leased to Jose (Joe) Faria who opened a nightclub, the Tarantella. Despite an unsavoury reputation which resulted in many complaints from local businessmen and residents, the nightclub operated for 21 years before closing in 1993. Its patrons were often blamed for vandalism in the city's west and heritage precinct though Mr Faria maintained most of the complaints were unjustified and the club had been victimised by some competing hoteliers. The building remained empty for two years until it became a bed and breakfast facility and was eventually acquired by Notre Dame University. The building was leased for student accommodation before housing the School of Medicine's planning team.

The heritage-listed building, constructed in the Federation Romanesque style, was built in two stages in 1903 - the façade and front section comprising a residence, office and a warehouse and later that year, additional warehouses at the rear. The owner, local investor William deLacey Bacon or his architect, E.H. Dean Smith, was influenced by the famous castles of Bavaria. In the heady days of the gold boom in WA a century ago, architects went out of their way to create distinguished or elaborate buildings to impress their clients or indulge themselves. The gold boom significantly changed the face of Fremantle with the construction of ornate buildings which reflected the prosperity and confidence of the time.

However, even now the Consulate building stands out, described in the book *Looking Around Perth: A guide to the architecture of Perth and surrounding towns* as 'highly individualistic and rugged...quite brutalistic.'

# Bizarre suicide marked a bank's early days

Western Australian Bank Building
22 High Street
Map Ref: 5

**O**n a summer's night in late January, 1893, a man was spotted in great distress as he walked down Mouat Street towards High Street, clutching his hand to his mouth. As The Inquirer and Daily News noted three days later: "Blood was profusely spurting through his fingers and the man was unable to speak."

Under the graphic headline - *A Man Attempts To Blow His Head Off With Dynamite* - the newspaper account of this extraordinary event detailed how a passerby, a Mr Bloom, tried to help by taking him to the chemist shop in the Western Australian Bank building at 22 High Street. However, Mr Mayhew, the chemist, said proper medical attention was needed. The remaining sequel to this saga saw the man taken to a doctors' surgery nearby and then, after police were called to assist, to the hospital casualty ward where, as the paper put it, "the unfortunate man expired."

It was later discovered that the victim of this bizarre suicide, a Swede named Frank Yensen, had apparently put a detonator cap in his mouth which, as The Inquirer described "blew off the top of his mouth and inflicted other serious injuries to which he eventually succumbed." A track of blood drops traced the origins of the incident back along Mouat Street to the corner of Phillimore Street.

*The Western Australian Bank around the time of the suicide. Note the dark area to the right of the building, which was probably then the chemist shop before being redesigned in 1903.*

The drama has some relevance to the rather unstable history of the Western Australian Bank, whose elegant new premises with the classical frontage on the corner of High and Mouat streets had been opened just the year before. Designed by the prominent Perth architect-soldier, Lieutenant-General Sir Talbot Hobbs, this splendid, purpose-built edifice had marble and ornamental tile foyers and polished cedar fittings, highlighted by a magnificent central staircase. Incorporated in the design was the chemist shop at its eastern end where the injured man was taken.

While banks are not generally colourful topics, the story behind the building at 22 High Street is an interesting insight into the commercial ebb and flow of a developing Western Australia. The Western Australian Bank was in a sense a breakaway bank from the original Bank of Western Australia started in 1837.

Indeed, historians comment that the State owes much to its foresighted policies, putting the development and progress of the community first.

Sadly, all good stories don't always have a happy ending. While by 1912 the bank's paid up capital had risen to £200,000, by the 1920s its former premier position was under severe attack from the larger national banks and, in 1927, directors recommended its sale to the Bank of New South Wales. It subsequently traded as a Westpac branch until 1999, when it was bought by the University of Notre Dame. Already, much of the ornate interior had been "modernised," including the removal of the staircase. The chemist's shop had been closed since 1903 when it became the bank manager's office.

Today, the building's classic exterior is classified by the National Trust, while its interior is home to the university's College of Health.

This occurred in 1841 when, after the WA Bank was taken over by the much larger Bank of Australasia, a group of dissatisfied shareholders decided to form a new one.

Clearly this was a tough task, given the competition, and the early moves to raise capital were not propitious. The plan was to launch the Western Australian Bank with capital of £5000 in fully paid shares but, when it opened, it had only 62 shareholders and a fully paid capital of around £2000. Initially, the bank's difficulties were further impacted by its competitor's access to its UK resources, providing local businesses with facilities for overseas trade. However, this was remedied in 1842 when the bank obtained a London agent and managed to undercut the other bank's discount rates. Then in 1845, during a depression, the Bank of Australasia closed its WA operations. From that point the WA bank grew and, particularly in the latter part of the century, was a leading player in the development of the colony.

The bank did not begin permanent operations in Fremantle until 1878, when it had an agency in Cliff Street for the collection of bills and cheques. After later moving to new quarters at 12 High Street, the directors decided bigger premises were needed and, in 1892, shifted to its stately new property at 22 High Street. During 1892-93 a depression forced the closure of many WA financial institutions, but the Western Australian Bank not only survived, but grew.

*WHEN Phillip Fawcett drove his horse and cart around the bank building corner on March 7, 1903, he failed to observe a street sign warning: Walk Your Horse Around The Corner. The Evening Courier reported that "Fawcett was charged with having driven around a corner at a pace faster than a walk." He was fined 10 shillings ($1), in those days a considerable sum.*

# Pioneer family's lasting link with Fremantle

Lionel Samson and Son Pty Ltd
Samson Building, 31 Cliff Street
Map Ref: 2
Samson House, corner of Ellen and Ord Streets
Map Ref: 38

The founders of Australia's **oldest** family business must have wondered what they had struck when they first set foot in the Swan River Colony in August 1829.

When brothers Lionel and William Samson arrived on the barque *Calista* five months after leaving England they found the authorities unprepared. No provision had been made for the *Calista* arrivals and they and their belongings were landed on the beach at Arthur Head. Their only shelter was the tents they had brought with them. However, the Samsons were undeterred by their poor reception. They had had the foresight to bring a substantial range of merchandise with them and quickly set about making a success of their venture 'down-under'. Within days of their arrival they had set up shop on the beach at Bathers Bay.

The Samsons were members of a prominent and wealthy English family. Both had been members of the London Stock Exchange and originally planned to emigrate to Canada. But Lionel's chance meeting in London with his friend, Captain James Stirling, persuaded him that WA provided better opportunities. Stirling had explored the area in 1827 and returned to establish the colony two years later.

Lionel and William Samson formed a partnership on arrival. A month later Lionel wrote to the Colonial Secretary that he intended to set up a store on his allotment in Mouat Street for the "disposal of various articles, including spirits" and that he was "desirous of obtaining a (liquor) licence to that effect."

The licence was soon granted - the first in the colony - which took effect from January 1,1830 and is still used today. In May Lionel was appointed the Fremantle postmaster, but the position was a financial burden to him because of his generosity in providing bags, sealing wax and string to settlers free of charge and providing tots of spirits for people waiting to have their mail sorted. He relinquished the position in 1832. In 1830 the Samsons moved from Mouat Street to nearby Cliff Street with the purchase of a stone cottage. This still stands within the company's headquarters and was Lionel's residence for much of his life.

A major problem for the brothers was the replenishment of stocks for their store and they found it necessary to charter ships and go as far as the Cape of Good Hope (now Capetown) in South Africa to purchase a wide range of merchandise. In 1839 they bought a schooner, *Elizabeth* (later wrecked in a storm at Bunbury) to trade between Fremantle, the Eastern Australian colonies and Asia. By 1844 they were among the main exporters of sheep, cattle, horses and dried fish to Mauritius and were involved in the export of sandalwood to Singapore and China.

The departure of William to South Australia in 1846 led to the dissolution of the brothers' partnership. Lionel carried on as a sole trader until his eldest son Michael joined him and the business was renamed Lionel Samson and Son in 1867. When Lionel died in 1878 his wife Fanny and her children ran the business, expanding the wine and spirits section. The first manager was appointed in 1897. The offices, warehouse and cellar built in

Cliff Street in 1898 are still the company's headquarters. The company now has extensive interests and almost 50 members of the Samson family are still company shareholders.

The family has a proud record of community service. Lionel was a long-serving member of the Legislative Council, the foundation chairman of the WA Chamber of Commerce, was at the forefront of the campaign to introduce convicts to solve the colony's serious labour and population problem and helped establish the game of cricket in the colony.

*Sir Frederick Samson in 1972, the year he retired as Mayor of Fremantle.*

Three Samsons have served as Fremantle Mayor, the best-known Sir Frederick Samson, the son of Michael, grandson of Lionel and a passionate advocate for the city and its heritage. Sir Fred was born in 1892 in the house his parents had built three years earlier. The house in Ellen Street, with the square tower, where he lived most of his life, now draws many visitors curious about its origins and its many interesting features and artifacts.

*Above & below: Samson House in Ellen Street where Sir Frederick was born, now draws many visitors.*

Sir Fred was educated in Fremantle before going to the University of Western Australia with the aim of becoming an engineer. However, his studies were interrupted by World War I, when he joined the airforce after being declared too short to enlist in the army. A cracked knee bone from an accident at home soon ended his war service and deciding not to pursue his studies, he got a job with a government department. After the war he became a partner in a surveying firm before starting his own real estate company.

Sir Fred's involvement with public affairs grew rapidly as a member of numerous local and State organisations. In 1936 he was elected to the Fremantle City Council and became mayor in 1951 - a position he held for 21 years until his retirement in 1972.

Sir Fred always said that Perth would not have existed if it weren't for the Port city. He was Fremantle's most outspoken advocate, whether in the company of a visiting businessman or the Queen. He involved himself across the board in activities affecting the progress of Fremantle and its people. And he was devoted to preserving its cultural identity, a stand which has won widespread gratitude ever since. Early in his local government career he was instrumental in establishing the industrial and housing area of O'Connor to provide jobs and homes for servicemen returning from World War II, the first such centre created by any Australian local council.

His determination to preserve Fremantle from the developers' bulldozers reached its highest point with the fight to save the old Lunatic Asylum and restore it as today's History Museum and Arts Centre.

The State Government wanted to knock it down but Sir Fred fought hard against the move. His final coup was winning the support of the Earl of Euston, then chairman of the National Trust of Great Britain who, after visiting the building, said it was the best example of colonial gothic architecture in Australia and should never be pulled down.

Sir Fred was knighted in 1962 in recognition of his services and became Fremantle's first honorary freeman seven years later. He died in 1974, aged 82.

The Samson family name lives on in the nearby Fremantle suburb of Samson and Point Samson in WA's north-west, named after Sir Fred's father. Another Samson to make a mark was Lionel's nephew Horace who worked in the family business before becoming the Government Draftsman and designing the colony's first postage stamps. His black swan stamps are now valuable collectors' items.

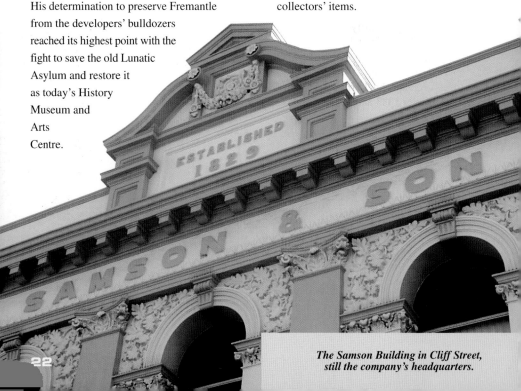

*The Samson Building in Cliff Street, still the company's headquarters.*

# Untimely deaths in a harsh land

## The Taylor Memorial Fountain
## Market Street, corner of Elder Street
## Map Ref: 32

The ornate and old-worldly Taylor Memorial Fountain, almost hidden behind a water pumping station and toilet opposite the Fremantle Railway Station, is an English father's tribute to two of his sons who died in a remote country, thousands of kilometres from home.

Erected in 1905, the inscription on the memorial reads simply: *Erected by John Taylor of London in memory of his sons Ernest and Peter who died in Western Australia.*

Over the years, the manner of their deaths has been variously attributed to dying of thirst on a desert expedition in WA, being murdered by Aborigines, trampled by camels and even more fancifully, cut down by maniacal oriental seamen.

John Taylor, a shipowner of the London firm, Bethell and Co, had a large family, including five adventurous sons. The eldest, John Foulkes Taylor, left home at the age of 17 and came to WA. He nearly died of thirst on an expedition with explorer and later politician John Forrest through the Kimberley region in 1883 and became a pioneer pastoralist.

Ernest Baines Taylor, the third son, arrived in WA in November, 1884, on the sailing ship *Darling Downs*, which was owned by his father. He took a job as a purser on *SS Natal*, a pioneer passenger steamer in the Fremantle-Singapore service, but a month short of his 22nd birthday, died in Fremantle in September, 1885.

The cause of his death is not recorded but it was reported that he had a frail constitution and had been ill for some time, possibly suffering from malaria. He collapsed and died in the Cliff Street home of Mr William Dalgety Moore, a prominent Fremantle businessman with links to the Taylor family as agent for Bethell and Co.

Peter Sothern Taylor, the fourth son, arrived in 1887 in *SS Elderslie*, another of their father's ships. Peter appears to have acted as his father's shipping agent in succession to older brother John. However, he met his death a long way from water - speared by Aborigines on Noonkanbah Station in the Kimberley in 1890. He had joined an expedition which went through the station in the remote north-west region. It is believed he might have unknowingly been on land sacred to the Aborigines.

In his will John Taylor provided funds for the monument to his sons. The Fremantle Council enthusiastically accepted the offer, recording that "drinking fountains are far too infrequent in Fremantle and the offer..........is not only appropriate but will be met with the grateful appreciation of the public".

The fountain, which cost about $400, was made by Doulton and Co Ltd in London and shipped to WA. Construction was supervised by a local architect. The memorial was designed on a water theme, with drinking places for birds, dogs, horses and humans. It was renovated in 1983 and added to the National Heritage list in 1996.

Moores Building
46 Henry Street
Map Ref: 6

**V**isitors to the contemporary arts gallery at the western end of Henry Street may not be aware that the building with its six spacious display areas is a legacy of one of WA's earliest 'merchant princes'. The Moores Building, with its magnificent limestone façade, is also a splendid example of Fremantle's determination to preserve its history through architectural restoration.

The Swan River Colony was only six years old when William Dalgety Moore was born in August 1835. His parents, Samuel and Dora Moore (née Dalgety) had arrived in the colony in April 1834 after a five-month voyage from England and built a family home in Middle Swan, east of Perth. Indeed, the Moore connection with WA had already begun in 1830, just a year after settlement, when George Fletcher Moore, one of Samuel's older brothers, had arrived and been appointed Advocate General, in charge of the colony's legal matters. While George Moore's contribution to those early years of settlement was considerable, his nephew, William, was to put the Moore stamp on the colony in a different way - through establishing W.D. Moore & Co, a corporate name that survives to this day.

*William Dalgety Moore*

William was only 13 when his father died in 1849, aged 46. As the eldest of five children, he quickly found work in the offices of the Surveyor General, John Septimus Roe. One imagines Uncle George may have brought some influence to help his young nephew but, if so, that would soon have dissipated because, in 1852,

*First wife,*
*Susannah (Monger) Moore*

*Second wife,*
*Annie (Gallop) Moore*

he resigned as Advocate General after a row with the Colonial Office and left the colony for good.

In 1855 William quit the office life and, nearly two years later, headed north to work on a cattle station in the Irwin River district. He later became the station manager. No doubt this change of direction, which lasted five years, provided valuable experience for a business future, along with excitement and romance. It was during this period he joined a group of explorers investigating the Murchison and Gascoyne areas, and married Susannah Monger, the daughter of another pioneering family. They wed in 1860 and, during 16 years of marriage, had 12 children.

The move to Fremantle came in 1862 when William went into business with his brother-in-law, John Monger, branching out on his own in 1867 to found W.D. Moore and Co. The general merchant business operated from a group of assorted buildings located at what is now 46 Henry Street. Originally the complex comprised a warehouse, factory, stables, offices and a family cottage, where the Moores first lived. The business grew rapidly from general wine and spirits merchants into a formidable range of commercial interests which included shipping, timber milling, flour milling, and the sale and distribution of a wide variety of much needed goods across the State. During the 1890s the company imported windmills from the USA, which both reinforced the ongoing connection with the pastoral area and led later to diversification as a major manufacturer of windmills.

The next two decades must have been extremely hectic and, one imagines, often stressful for the Moore family. Three of the couple's 12 children had died before Susannah herself passed away in 1876. In 1879, William married 26-year-old Annie Gallop, who subsequently bore him a further six children. During this period the head of family had also been increasingly involved in the colony's civic and political fortunes, representing Fremantle's interests on various government committees. As well as these and other responsibilities, he was the first president of the Fremantle Chamber of Commerce.

It was during this period - in 1899 at the height of the WA gold rush - that the classical façade was added to the Henry Street premises, to bring cohesion to the clutter of buildings behind.

In 1902, William moved to Woodside, a stately family mansion he had built on 56 ha of land in East Fremantle, where he lived until his death in 1910. He had already in 1900 sold the business to his son, George Frederick Moore. Settlement of William's estate took 16 years to complete before the property was sold, first to a doctor who turned it into a private hospital and, in 1951, to the State Government, after which Woodside became the maternity hospital still there today.

Meanwhile, the Henry Street building remained the headquarters of W.D. Moore & Co until 1955, when it moved to its current premises in nearby O'Connor. By then its operations had changed substantially from general merchandising to engineering and manufacturing. The Fremantle City Council bought the property in 1986 and, with the help of a Federal Government America's Cup Grant, began a progressive restoration program completed in 1996. The project received an award of merit from the Royal Australian Institute of Architects and the building was given heritage status.

# The Aboriginal connection - troubled times in early days

**T**he white settlement of the Swan River Colony was initially treated cautiously by Aborigines who inhabited and used the Fremantle area - but it wasn't long before a clash of cultures led to serious trouble.

The arrival of the first settlers in 1829 was not the first contact between Aborigines - with a connection to the land going back 60,000 years - and Europeans. There had been earlier contact with explorers and traders blown off course. In the 1800s, which saw increased British and French interest in Australia's west coast, one European observer described Aborigines he had seen as very shy.

But the perceived shyness was probably more wariness of strangers who had different dress and attitudes. Renowned anthropologist Ronald Berndt believed Aborigines thought white Europeans were the spirits of the returned dead, which would explain their desire to keep their distance. By the time of Captain James Stirling's 1827 Swan River expedition it was noted that Aborigines seemed angry at the invasion of their territory. So before 28-year-old Captain Charles Howe Fremantle arrived on *Challenger* in 1829 to prepare for British settlement he was already uneasy about the native inhabitants. He understood them to be 'troublesome, rather warlike and savage to the utmost extent' and, apprehensive about potential hostility, he brought gifts to gain their friendship.

On his second contact with Aborigines he heard shouting and saw some running along the hills and towards the river bank. Assuming they were friendly he rowed to shore. "One came to the boat and I gave him a biscuit which he eat immediately and he made signs for my hat, which being very old I gave him and he gave me in return a bit of string with which his hair was bound around, as I wish'd to shew him that it was our intention to be friendly."

Aborigines had lived in the area or used it as a food source and significant tribal meeting place for thousands of years. Swamps where Mouat and Henry Streets are now were high in plant and animal life. Fresh water was obtained from shallow wells. Cantonment Hill provided elevation and shelter. At low tide the limestone bar at the mouth of the Swan River provided the only crossing on the river between the coast and Heirisson Island at Perth. The people who lived there knew the ancient history of the area including how the land had once extended past Rottnest, 20 kilometres west. Aborigines from far and wide gathered for feasts and ceremonies.

However, once settlement began the good relations Charles Fremantle had established with local Aborigines soon deteriorated. With the loss of significant traditional land to settlers and the realisation that the disruption to their way of life was permanent, Aboriginal resistance began, led by local tribal chief, Midgegooroo, and his son Yagan. In December 1831, some Aborigines raiding a potato patch were ambushed and a friend of Yagan shot dead. In a revenge raid a farm worker was speared to death. Six months later a group led by Yagan ambushed two farm labourers and killed one. Yagan was proclaimed an outlaw with a bounty on his head. Earlier, Midgegooroo had thrown a spear at a Fremantle storeman because he was not satisfied with the amount of biscuits he had been given.

In October 1832 Yagan and two friends were captured and sent to exile, under supervision, on offshore Carnac Island. Two months later they seized an unattended dinghy and rowed 8km to the mainland and freedom. In April 1833 Yagan's brother was shot dead while breaking into a store in Fremantle. The following day Yagan, Midgegooroo and about 40 others ambushed a supply wagon heading out of Fremantle and fatally speared two brothers. Midgegooroo was captured in May, imprisoned in Perth and later executed by firing squad.

Yagan survived until July when he and a companion were shot at Guildford, east of Perth, by teenage brothers William and James Keates. William was speared by other Aborigines who had heard the shots. James escaped by swimming the Swan River and after claiming a reward left for Tasmania. Yagan's head was hacked from his body and taken to England. It was not returned to WA until 1997. Yagan had been spared the death penalty after his 1832 capture by successfully claiming he was a prisoner of war. He told the court: "You came to our country. You have driven us from our haunts and disturbed us in our occupations. As we walk in our own country we are fired upon by the white men. Why should the white man treat us so?"

Important to Aborigines in the early days of settlement - though for different reasons - were the Round House and the whaling station. Yagan had been locked up in the Round House before being exiled to Carnac Island and was reported to have returned to "exchange civilities with his late keeper." Relatives of Aboriginal prisoners went at night to talk to them from outside the walls. It became notorious as the last place Aboriginal prisoners were kept before being taken to Rottnest where many died in custody. The whaling station in Bathers Bay dealt in what had always been a favourite Aboriginal food - whalemeat. Before settlement the stranding of whales had been an occasion for big gatherings, feasting and merriment.

Within 10 years of settlement the Aboriginal population at Fremantle had been severely reduced by violence, alcohol and disease though there were times even in the 1860s when they still outnumbered whites. However, a severe measles epidemic in 1883 is said to have killed many Aborigines in the Fremantle area. Today, families of Aboriginal descent have made a significant contribution to the Fremantle community.

*Yagan, a free spirit immortalised in bronze, was spared the death penalty after arguing that he was a prisoner of war. The statue is on Heirisson Island, Perth.*

# Law library's links to early merchant family

Bateman Buildings, University of Notre Dame
Croke Street
Map Ref: 7

**I**t is hard to believe that at the high water mark the Indian Ocean once lapped the foundations of buildings in Croke Street now occupied by the University of Notre Dame.

Reclamation has since pushed the shoreline well away from the area so it takes some imagination to picture the era when cargo from sailing ships anchored at the nearby jetty was off-loaded onto small boats, taken directly to the Bateman warehouses and hoisted to the top floor.

Tangible reminders of that era are the top-floor hoists which remain on the outside of the 1870s buildings. And when the building was being transformed from a derelict warehouse to the University's College of Law - a triumph of architectural

*A custard powder mill still in situ in a lecture room of Notre Dame's Graduate School of Law.*

and construction ingenuity - seaweed was found under the flooring and deeper excavations revealed seagrass remains. But while the buildings remain, the Bateman family's long business link with Fremantle is virtually forgotten, a victim of corporate plays in the heady entrepreneurial 1980s.

John Bateman, a 40-year-old former London silk mercer, arrived in the Swan River Colony with his wife and five children on the schooner *Medina* in 1830 and laid the foundations of Western Australia's second-oldest company. Bateman, like many other middle-class English people of the time, had been caught up in "Swan River Fever" and had optimistic expectations of a new life in remote WA. But it was tougher than he and others had imagined. Although he was a licensed storekeeper, by 1833 he also held several other positions, including schoolmaster, Magistrates' Clerk and assistant Harbour Master, to support his family. In 1835 he was appointed the first Postmaster at Fremantle. He once commented: "Business has been so bad lately that for days together we do not take one shilling a day." During the hard times he once had to ask the Colonial Secretary for a grant of two bushels of wheat.

The years following his arrival had been difficult, often because of the shortage of supplies from England. But while many newcomers left the colony, disappointed by its slow progress, Bateman battled on.

By 1834 he had a "well-built" store and dealt in a variety of provisions.

The family's business links with the ocean began in 1837 when Bateman became secretary of the Fremantle Whaling Company which built the tunnel under the Round House to transport whale oil from the processing point to the town. On his death in 1855 the business was continued by his sons John and Walter and from 1857 the business became known as J. and W. Bateman. By 1859 business had strengthened and the brothers had become the colony's leading importers and exporters with their own fleet of sailing ships which operated in coastal and overseas trade. Bateman ships travelled to China and Singapore with sandalwood and Mauritius with horses, returning with produce such as sugar and tea demanded by the growing colony. They also supplied water for ships from their private well, leading the Harbour Master to complain in 1864: "The present system of supplying water is by means of casks filled at Mr Bateman's

well and boated to the ships in his cargoboats only.....this process is dilatory and expensive...."

John Bateman jun., who bought his brother's share in the business in 1872, became the biggest shipowner in WA and the crew of one of his ships, *Flying Foam*, is credited with finding the first pearls to be discovered in Australia - in the Nickol Bay area in WA's north-west. However, with the advent of steamships and the demise of sailing ships (coupled with the expensive loss of several of their ships) shipping ceased to become a primary source of income and the family turned to other enterprises such as hardware and wholesale groceries.

*Where the boats pulled up in Croke Street... Above: Note the jutting beam, top left, used to hoist goods aloft from boats which brought goods to the edge of the Indian Ocean marked by the brickline at the front of the building (below)*

The company opened a shop in Perth in 1910 and by 1913 had premises in Fremantle with frontage onto Henry, Croke and Mouat Streets, covering about 1.2ha of land. The 60,000sq.ft of floor space included a warehouse and a manufacturing department responsible for the preparation of coffee essences, condiments, baking powder and various other groceries. Apart from being wholesale grocers, the Batemans were also shipping and insurance brokers, wine and spirit merchants and general ironmongers. Later expansion saw stores in Albany, Bunbury, Geraldton and Kalgoorlie.

The company was incorporated in 1919. Although it diversified it was predominantly a hardware company and remained largely a family company until the 1980s when corporate plays saw it fall into other hands and later delisted by the Stock Exchange.

The Bateman family played a leading role in Fremantle's development. The original John Bateman served on the Town Trust (today's City Council). His son Walter was elected to the seat of Normanton in Fremantle's first Parliamentary elections and the third John Bateman was a member of the Fremantle Town Council, chairman of the Fremantle Harbour Trust and president of the Fremantle Chamber of Commerce (1895-1900) at a time when the discovery of gold and the construction of Fremantle Harbour brought unparalleled expansion to the port. John Bateman (the fourth) was also President of the Chamber on four occasions between 1918 and 1943.

Mary Ann Bateman, wife of the first John Bateman, returned to England in 1858 three years after her husband's death. She lived to 1866, regretting the 1830 decision to move to the fledgling colony. The Bateman name lives on not far from Fremantle via a major suburban road and a suburb both named after the family.

# Where law students can act with great credibility

Old Courthouse
Marine Terrace
Map Ref: 8

**L**aw students at Fremantle's University of Notre Dame are specially privileged. They are the only ones in Australia and, possibly, any university city in the world to have on campus a real courtroom in which to practice their skills. This is the courthouse in Marine Terrace opposite the Esplanade which, most observers would note, usually seems quiet and unoccupied.

Not so during semester when the courthouse frequently becomes the lively setting for "moots", or mock trials, providing students with an authentic environment in which to get into the swing of their future careers.

The light brown building with its smooth, stucco walls and striking two-door entrance on the corner of Mouat Street attracts much attention from passers-by and sightseers. Its history is an integral part of the emerging port city's early growth spreading outwards and eastwards from its origins near Bathers Beach.

It is this area, the historical west end of Fremantle, where the university chose to create a scatter of colleges by buying or leasing and restoring some 15 per cent of available real estate. Much of it, left high and dry by the big ebb of port activity, faced an otherwise uncertain future, the buildings derelict and in disrepair. Today, those buildings are preserved and revitalised and the students have brought a new dimension to the community.

The University of Notre Dame Australia was founded in 1990 and admitted its first students in January 1992. The entire campus in Fremantle then comprised 35 students and 12 staff, housed in a restored warehouse at 19 Mouat Street. Today, there is also a campus at Broome on the North-West coast and the overall numbers have risen dramatically to more than 3500 students and 320 staff. The university now occupies a number of historic Fremantle buildings spread mostly through six blocks bounded by Phillimore Street and Marine Terrace (north-south) and Cliff and Henry Streets. Among them are former hotels, such as Cleopatra and the P & O Hotel, the early Bateman buildings along Croke Street, the old Drill Hall and the consulate building which became a nightclub. Some of these landmarks are dealt with separately in this book. All are open to the public on a pre-arranged guided tour basis (see opposite).

Just like the courthouse, the buildings have been restored as closely as possible to their original identity, making for peaceful and absorbing places for study and learning, often in spacious halls beneath lofty ceilings and timber beams. The courthouse itself is neither lofty nor spacious, which was one of the early criticisms after it was built in 1884 at a cost of £930. The entire courtroom is 12 metres long by eight metres wide and, in the days when the court was sitting, the elevated magistrate's bench took up more than a third of the room, leaving restricted standing space for the public.

*Picture: Craig Kinder, ƒ22 photography*

*Practising their skills... Notre Dame law students conducting "moots" in an authentic environment.*

The courthouse was built to take over from two earlier ones near the Round House which had served the community consecutively from 1835 to 1881. From the outset, however, when the official opening was delayed because the Governor was held up grouse shooting on Rottnest Island, it had a chequered career. Indeed, after only 13 years' operation as a court, police station and lock-up, the booming population from gold fever - along with a consequent increase in crime rates - made it hopelessly inadequate, and a new courthouse was built where it still stands, but no longer in use, in Henderson Street.

From that point the building had a chameleon-like career, reflecting the needs of the time. From 1897 it was occupied jointly by the Fremantle Water Supply and the police. At the end of 1918 it became a temporary home for war-ravaged European migrants, then, during the 1920s and 30s, the office of the Public Works Department. After remaining empty for nearly two decades, the small building was again put to use, first as an independent home for alcoholics, then a night shelter for homeless men, a Salvation Army hostel and, finally, a Uniting Church food distribution centre.

In December 1997 the University of Notre Dame signed a 10-year lease with the State Government on the condition that it faithfully restored the much beleaguered building. This included refurbishing the interior with the original benching from Perth's Beaufort Street Magistrates Courts. The building was reopened in 1998 and, ever since, has been used for different, appropriate university meetings, among which, particularly, has been the ongoing and valuable student reenactment of its original function and purpose. In 2002 the State Government vested the courthouse in the university in perpetuity.

*NOTE: The University of Notre Dame welcomes visitors wishing to book a guided tour, or attend its annual Open Day. Enquiries on 9433 0692, or email communityrelations@nd.edu.au.*

# Batavia's voyage to disaster

**The wrecking of Batavia** off the West Australian coast in 1629 - and its savage and bloody aftermath - is one of the greatest dramas and tragedies in Australia's history. Centuries later it was remarked that by comparison the Mutiny on the Bounty was an anaemic tale.

Batavia, which ran aground in darkness on Morning Reef in the Wallibi Group of the Abrolhos Islands, off Geraldton, was the first of the Verenigde Oostindische Compagnie (VOC) ships to be lost off the Australian coast. The story of the wreck and the subsequent treachery and murders has been the subject of numerous books - the first published in Amsterdam in 1648 - and a magnificent display in the WA Museum's world-renowned Shipwreck Galleries.

Batavia, the flagship of a convoy, left Holland in October 1628 under the command of Francisco Pelsaert, bound for the VOC's trading centre Batavia (now Jakarta, Indonesia). A total of 316 people, including women and children, were on board the ship laden with merchandise, jewels and coins. Plans for the mutiny, led by under-merchant Jeronimus Cornelisz and supported by some officers and crew, were already underway when the ship, which had become separated from the rest of the convoy, struck the reef in June 1629. Forty people drowned but the rest managed to reach the nearby small islands. Little water or food was saved from the wreck.

Pelsaert, skipper Ariaen Jacobsz and 46 crew took Batavia's two small open boats in search of water. The trip was unsuccessful and it was decided to continue to Batavia - about 1200 nautical miles away - to get help to rescue the castaways. In the meantime Cornelisz put himself in charge of the island, planning to capture the rescue ship when it arrived. He then arranged for most of the ship's soldiers to be taken to another island on the pretext of searching for water. Leaving them stranded, Cornelisz appointed himself 'Governor' and ordered his supporters to slaughter all those opposed to the mutiny.

However, his plan went awry when the stranded soldiers managed to find fresh water and survive on birds, seals and wallabies. Hearing of the massacres on the other island they built a shelter and waited for Cornelisz to attack. They repulsed the first attack and captured Cornelisz on the second. When Pelsaert returned three months later he was told of the mutiny and was able to quickly capture Cornelisz's supporters. One hundred and twenty five men, women and children had been murdered and 20 had died from disease or illness. Only 74 survived to eventually return to Batavia.

Retribution was swift. Pelsaert brought the mutineers to trial on the spot. Cornelisz was hanged after having both his hands cut off. Others were executed, keelhauled or lashed. Two were banished to the mainland opposite and nothing heard of them again. Pelsaert was able to salvage all but one of the 12 chests crammed with coins which went down with Batavia. But this was not enough to restore his standing with the VOC, the biggest trading concern in the world in the 17th and early 18th centuries with Batavia as its trade centre. He was heavily criticised - as the highest in command - for not staying with the shipwreck survivors. This, combined with rumours that he had engaged in private trade against VOC rules, led to his rapid decline in the company - and his health - and he died in 1630.

Three other VOC ships - Vergulde Draeck (Gilt Dragon, 1656), Zuytdorp (1712) and Zeewijk (1727) - were also wrecked off the WA coast on the way to the East Indies to trade for valuable silks, spices and other goods. The wrecks lay undisturbed until the 1960s when maritime archaeologists began to survey, research and excavate the sites. A highlight of the Galleries' displays is the reconstruction of a section of *Batavia's* hull. The remains of *Batavia* were excavated in the 1970s and rebuilt after lengthy treatment by the Museum's Department of Materials Conservation. The timber was protected on the sea-bed by a cargo of sandstone blocks intended as a gateway for the Castle of Batavia and now reassembled to form an impressive portico façade. Also displayed is the skeleton of one of the people murdered on the Abrolhos. The stories of the other three ships - equally absorbing but far less dramatic - are told in the Dutch Wrecks Gallery. Another gallery is devoted to *SS Xantho*, WA's first coastal steamer, which sunk at Port Gregory within months of her arrival in the 1870s.

The 12,890km WA coastline, which varies from ragged, rocky reefs at the base of huge cliffs to long sandy beaches, has ended as a graveyard for a host of wrecked ships. Apart from the Dutch ships most other wrecks were sailing ships bringing settlers to WA and steamers bringing more immigrants and materials from England. Several were lost off Rottnest Island and on the approaches to Fremantle.

The Shipwreck Galleries is recognised as the foremost maritime archaeology museum in the southern hemisphere and one of the few museums in the world specifically devoted to the preservation and display of maritime archaeological material. It is in premises built as a Commissariat store between 1851 and 1862 mainly with convict labour. In 1878 the building was converted into a Customs House and Bonded Warehouse and was later used by various Government departments before becoming the WA Maritime Museum in 1977. In front of the Cliff Street entrance is a small area of the original Yorkshire flagstones brought as ballast in early ships and used as paving. The Shipwreck Galleries is visited by 220,000 people a year, most from outside WA.

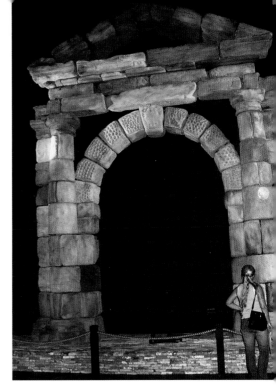

*The sandstone blocks that never reached their intended destination as a gateway for the Castle of Batavia.*

# Fishermen gave port its cultural identity

Fremantle Fishing Boat Harbour
Mews Road
Map Ref: 10

**W**hen 23-year-old Calogero Basile arrived in Fremantle in 1905, he was not to know that a century later his name, along with hundreds of others, would be inscribed on a monument as one of the founders of what is today a billion-dollar fishing industry.

A photograph of Basile and 15 other well-dressed Italian fishermen gives little indication of their occupation. The image, reproduced in bronze, is displayed along with the names of early and more recent fishermen at the impressive memorial jetty at Fremantle Fishing Boat Harbour.

Like those before him and those who followed, Basile's intent was to make a new life away from the generally poverty-ridden southern half of Italy. The first substantial group of men had arrived a few years earlier from the village of Capo d'Orlando in the north-east of Sicily, to be closely followed by fishermen from Molfetta on the Adriatic coast of Italy. Like Calogero Basile, they often left their families behind, hoping to make enough money to resettle them later in Australia.

Indeed, Calogero Basile made three trips to Western Australia, staying and working over a period of several years before returning to Sicily for good. In the process he was first accompanied by a younger brother and, later, by a son, Antonino, who stayed on and made his life in Australia. His nephew, Claude Basile, was the family's third-generation fisherman in Fremantle, now retired from active fishing but still involved in aspects of the industry and promoting its heritage.

Italians had been coming to WA individually since the colony was founded in 1829, but it was around the turn of the century, partly encouraged by the gold rush as well as deteriorating living conditions in Europe, that organised ethnic groups of fishermen were formed, the Capo d'Orlandans and the Molfettese being the major two. These were followed progressively in the latter half of the 19th century by people from many countries, including Greece, Croatia, Germany, Spain, Scandinavia, Estonia, Portugal and Great Britain. Their convergence on Fremantle in time led to establishing a major fishing industry and, not least, the port city's strong cultural identity as a place of many nationalities.

From the outset, fishing for a living was a tough life. Initially, new arrivals either lived on the boats or in small shacks on the beach (the first of these were built from flotsam and jetsam washed ashore). By the turn of the century some 150 Italians were trying to make a living this way, from the waters

*Left: Capo d'Orlando fishermen, Fremantle 1905. Calogero Basile back row, second from left.*
*Right: Claude Basile, third-generation fisherman with the bronze sculpture of a fisherman.*

of Cockburn Sound. They worked, often day and night sevens days a week, operating as separate groups from Rockingham, Point Peron just south of Fremantle and from Fremantle. Their catches were mostly herring, mullet, garfish and snapper, which were sold variously, either direct to the public or to hawkers and dealers, before the Fremantle Fish Market was opened on South Jetty in 1908.

With the implementation of organised marketing, the fishermen lost control of the sale - and pricing - of the fish they caught. As the governing body and legitimate auctioneer, the Fremantle Municipal Council charged high rates for use and commissions whilst the wholesalers were tough businessmen with high overheads and investments. In short, the fishermen were in the hands of the buyers and overt price-fixing, an inequitable situation exacerbated by fluctuating demand and supply which was to persist for several decades. Consequently, while the fishermen did not always choose to sell their fish legitimately through the market, black marketeering became rife while many struggled to make a living.

World War II created another black hole for the Italians many of whom, suspected of being "aliens", were banned from fishing. Some had their boats confiscated, others were interned in labour camps. While there were those who did quite well selling on the black market after 1942 when food was in shorter supply, the struggle by the majority to reach some semblance of equity continued after the war.

It all came to a head in 1947 after years of heartbreak, intermittent strike action, lobbying and official inquiries. In July that year the fishermen went on strike again to highlight the injustice of pricing policies and, at last, there was a breakthrough. On August 9 the Fremantle Fishermen's Co-operative Society held its first official meeting as a legally incorporated body, at last turning the tide in favour of the fishermen. During that year the first lobsters were exported, mainly to the USA, beginning what was to become a multi-million dollar export industry. By the 1970s the co-operative society had an annual turnover of more than $32 million.

For the likes of Claude Basile, who came to Fremantle from Capo d'Orlando in 1952 as a seven-year-old with his mother and younger brother and sister, the groundwork was already in place to build a successful future - first with his father, Salvatore, who had come to WA two years earlier to set up for his family, and ultimately as a successful fisherman in his own right.

Today, much of the Fremantle and broader community bears the names of its pioneer fishing ancestry. Names like Cicerello and Kailis, Ianello and Merlino, Parentich and Martinovich, Casserely and Poole, Porcelli and De Ceglie. More than 600 fishermen from 12 nations are identified on the memorial jetty at Fishing Boat Harbour, a fine tribute to so many who worked so hard and often perilously against the odds to build an industry now applauded internationally.

# America's Cup triumph began at this old jetty

Fremantle Fishing Boat Harbour
Map Ref: 39

**A**t the southern end of the Fremantle Fishing Boat Harbour is an old jetty where Fremantle's journey with the America's Cup began. A few hundred metres north is an unpretentious boat yard where it finished.

In 1970 a young Fremantle entrepreneur, Alan Bond, and his eccentric but brilliant friend and yacht designer Bob Miller, climbed on to a large white yacht in a boat yard at City Island, New York. They were in the United States to compete in the famous Newport to Bermuda yacht race with Bond's yacht, the Miller-designed *Apollo*. The yacht they had cheekily boarded was *Valiant*, a new but ultimately unsuccessful candidate for the defence of the America's Cup held earlier that year off Newport, Rhode Island. The men were interrupted by New York Yacht Club member Vic Romagna, who gave them a sound ticking-off for trespassing on *Valiant*.

Bond reacted by asking what was the big deal and what was the America's Cup anyway? Miller gave him a short history of the world's oldest sporting competition, to which his response was that he would build his own 12-metre yacht and come back and win it off them. What appeared to be a bit of bravado, turned out to be the starting point of a saga that was to last the next 17 years and, along the way, change Fremantle for ever.

Bond's first move was to buy the 12-metre yachts owned by Sir Frank Packer, the Sydney-based media mogul, who had already mounted two unsuccessful attempts to win the "Auld mug", as the America's Cup was affectionately known. *Gretel* and *Gretel II* were shipped to Fremantle and housed at the small jetty upon which a simple shed was built to store sails and spares. The yachts were sailed off Fremantle by amateur crews from local yacht clubs before the project was moved to a new marina and yachting complex built at Two Rocks, 100 kms north of Fremantle.

Bond's first attempt to win the Cup took place in 1974 when he challenged with the world's first aluminium 12-metre yacht, *Southern Cross*. He was roundly thrashed 4-0 but was back in 1977 with a new yacht, *Australia*, with the same result. In 1980

Bond returned to Newport for the third time with a modified *Australia*. Once again he beat all-comers to win the right to challenge but failed at the last hurdle, losing the Cup match to the superb American yacht *Freedom*, sailed by yachting legend Dennis Connor. The score was 4 - 1. Bond after three challenges had finally won a Cup race.

In 1983 Alan Bond was back in Newport but this time he had an ace up his sleeve. Bob Miller, now named Ben Lexcen, had designed a radical new 12-metre, *Australia II*. She featured an upside down winged keel that gave her incredible manoeuvrability, stability and hydrodynamic performance. There were many other subtle differences with her on-board electronics, mast, rigging and sail design. In addition Bond's team were now hardened veterans, many of whom had been involved in all three previous challenges. They were no longer happy to simply compete in the Cup. They were hungry for the ultimate prize.

During the summer of racing off Newport, *Australia II* swept the other six challengers aside and then faced off against the US defender *Liberty*, once again helmed by Dennis Connor.

The seven America's Cup races held over two weeks in Newport in September 1983 have since become a part of Australian folklore. *Australia II* lost the first two races due to breakdowns but won the third. She lost the next to be 3 - 1 down but came back and won races five and six to level the series at 3 - 3. The showdown was set for September 26.

*Australia II* won the start but was soon passed by *Liberty* who literally sailed away and at one stage was estimated to be two minutes in front - a huge margin. A wind shift put *Australia II* within a minute

*Above: Where it all began. The bow of **Gretel** can be seen (right) at the old jetty which is still there today. The shed has since been removed.*

*Right: Alan Bond joins the crew of **Australia II** after winning race 3 at Newport. Directly in front of him is relaxed skipper John Bertrand and, fourth from right, John Longley.*

AUSTR

at the start of the second last leg. While the world watched, *Australia II* picked another shift and with a superior spinnaker set, crept past to round the last mark 21 seconds in front. She clamped an iron cover on *Liberty* and finished 41 seconds in front to break the longest winning streak in sport - an extraordinary 132 years - and take the America's Cup to Fremantle.

In the period between the successful challenge and the defence in 1987, the sporting world was focused on Fremantle. Capital, both public and private flooded into the port city. Infrastructure that had had little spent on it for years, was upgraded. Heritage buildings found new life and were restored. Businesses were established, property values soared and Fremantle was put on the world map. As one commentator put it: *"The America's Cup started a party which has never stopped."*

Unfortunately success was short-lived. Dennis Connor returned with *Stars and Stripes* and beat the other twelve challengers in a series of spectacular races that spanned six months in the waters off Fremantle. Finally, he clean swept the 9-race series for the Cup 5 - 0 against the Australian defender *Kookaburra III* and took the Cup to San Diego.

Bond built two new yachts, *Australia III* and *Australia IV*, but for the first time in his involvement with the Cup failed to win the right to compete in the final match. The Bond defence was housed at the northern end of Mews Road in the Fremantle Fishing Boat Harbour in buildings that were later demolished to build the large white ship shed for the construction of the replica of *HMB Endeavour.*

Next door in Freedom Marine's yard, Dennis Connor campaigned his successful *Stars and Stripes* yachts. A little further to the north, next to today's Little Creatures Brewery, was the *Kookaburra* camp. On the other side and in adjacent Challenger and Success Harbours, a total of seventeen challenging and defending teams campaigned their boats and dreamt of America's Cup glory.

All of these teams built large sheds and cranes to campaign the yachts but all have been demolished, so today it is hard to see any evidence of the huge events surrounding the first defence of the America's Cup beyond American shores. Ironically, the little jetty where it all started is the only one of these facilities that remains virtually untouched.

*\*Australia II* is on display at the WA Maritime Museum.

# This *Endeavour* lived up to its name

WA Maritime Musum Shipwreck Galleries
Cliff Street
Map Ref: 9

**V**isitors to the Maritime Museum's Shipwreck Galleries may well wonder why the splendid glass display cases containing various artifacts and models of sailing ships are supported, somewhat incongruously, by bulky uprights of rough timber. There is no indication that these vertical stumps of pink-coloured Oregon were, in another place, part of a momentous event in the history of Fremantle.

It was a December afternoon in 1993. The occasion was the launch of *Endeavour*, a replica of the ship commanded by Lieutenant James Cook when he discovered the east coast of Australia in 1770. And the timber? It constituted the launching cradle, or poppet, from which *Endeavour* made its historic entry into the water that day.

Thursday, December 9, did not go precisely to plan. In fact, the ship was launched a few minutes earlier than anticipated, almost wrecking the critical moment of Channel 9's national television coverage of the event. Fortunately, the network was able to interrupt its scheduled commercial break and get the shot of *Endeavour* as the ropes were cut and she slid into the water - just in the nick of time.

Formalities had moved along more quickly than expected that day, including the early arrival of eminent botanist Dr Adrienne Clark to christen the ship, and the service that followed. As project leader John Longley said later, *"The service was a largely religious one and, like a wedding, once it started you didn't stop. You didn't look at your watch. It just went quicker than expected."*

The launch of *Endeavour* and its subsequent commissioning successfully ended a long and problem-ridden saga which had begun nearly six years earlier when the project was conceived. *Endeavour* was to be a $13 million bicentennial gift to the nation from the Bond Corporation.

However, plans went awry when the company ran into financial trouble after spending more than $8 million on the project. A Japanese company, Yoshiya, took over the sponsorship but later also discontinued its funding.

For eight months work came to a standstill, the hull of the replica remaining largely untouched on the site of the 1987 America's Cup Defence headquarters in Mews Road. Then, towards the end of 1991, shipwrights were back on the job with renewed funding generated via the formation of HM Bark Endeavour Ltd, a non-profit foundation. The foundation had already raised $2.35 million towards a $6 million shortfall, and would continue seeking individual donations and sponsorships in Australia, Britain and New Zealand - the countries with special links to the original *HMB Endeavour*. Much hard work and dedication to the cause ultimately won the day and, while the original launch timetable had been put back, the ship's construction continued without further interruption.

There were many mixed emotions among the huge crowd which gathered to farewell *Endeavour* when she set sail for the Australian National Maritime Museum in Sydney, her permanent home, one Sunday in October 1994. For the next 19 months the ship would traverse the eastern seaboard and New Zealand, before returning for a winter sojourn on public exhibition in Fremantle Fishing Boat Harbour. In mid-October 1996, the ship left Fremantle again - this time bound for England via Durban, St Helena, Ascension Island, Tenerife and Madeira - arriving in London on March 26, 1997.

*Endeavour* has sailed between Sydney and Whitby, the Yorkshire town where the original ship, a collier called *Earl of Pembroke*, was built in 1764. The ship was renamed *HMB Endeavour* three years later when the Royal Navy bought her out of trade before Cook embarked on his historic circumnavigation of the world.

*Picture: Richard Polden, The Sunday Times*

*Soon after the successful launch on December 9, 1993, which did not go entirely to plan*

Unlike the use of oak and elm in construction of the original ship, *Endeavour* is built from Australian hardwoods, including jarrah from the south-west of WA which was selected for the frames and planking below the waterline.

Fremantle's expertise and craftsmanship in boat-building as well as in replicating historic sailing ships have won the port city worldwide acclaim. While *Endeavour* may hold an extra special place in that respect, two other sailing ships - the training ship *Leeuwin* and the small but equally historic *Duyfken* - are also both splendid outcomes of people's determination to achieve difficult and costly goals.

As a consequence, history can be relived by bringing the past to the present. More importantly, perhaps, hundreds of young people are able to build their confidence and a sense of community by joining ship and experiencing the thrills and adventure of voyaging in local waters.

*Where it was built... the former America's Cup headquarters in Mews Road*

*The oregon timber base of this Endeavour model display was part of the launching cradle for the real thing.*

# A curious commemoration of controversial killings

Maitland Brown Memorial
Esplanade Reserve
Map Ref: 11

**F** **remantle is a curious venue** for the controversial Maitland Brown Memorial - also known as the Explorers' Monument - because the incident it commemorates has no substantial link to the port city.

And Brown's link with Fremantle was also relatively minor. He had spent some childhood years there but for most of his life lived at Champion Bay near Geraldton, some 500km north of Fremantle.

Brown - pastoralist, explorer, magistrate, politician and merchant and the uncle of Edith Dircksley Cowan, the first female member of any Parliament in Australia - was born to a pioneering farming family near York in 1843.

The family relocated to Fremantle in 1852 when his father, Thomas, took up his appointment as resident magistrate. At the age of 15 Maitland Brown joined his elder brother Kenneth on the property his family had established at Champion Bay. Three years later he was a member of Frank Gregory's exploration expedition to the north-west of Western Australia and is credited with saving Gregory's life. Gregory named a river after him near present-day Dampier.

In 1865 Frederick Panter, James Harding and Henry Goldwyer had been sent to survey country south of Roebuck Bay (site of present-day Broome). The expedition had been expected to take 14 days but on the fourth day the men were killed near La Grange Bay by local Aborigines. After nothing had been heard from the group after 60 days the Government organised a search party and Brown, a friend of Harding, who had also been on the Gregory expedition, volunteered to lead it.

Brown found the explorers' bodies at Boola Boola and believed they had been murdered in their sleep. Two local Aborigines, who had been forced to act as guides, were shot in the back as they tried to escape. Two days later Brown and his party began searching for the explorers' killers.

Accounts of what happened next differ. Brown said that his group was ambushed. Others say that he rode into an Aboriginal camp. What is not in dispute is that a battle ensued. At least six Aborigines were killed and 12 badly wounded though other reports have put the number killed much higher. The final incident came when two Aboriginal captives leapt over the side of Brown's boat. One drowned, the other escaped and the remaining prisoners were released.

Brown brought the explorers' bodies back to Perth, received a public tribute of thanks from the Government and at the age of 22 was appointed a Justice of the Peace. The following year he was appointed a magistrate, the youngest person to be offered the position in WA. He became a member of State Parliament at the age of 27 and at one stage was touted as the person most likely to become WA's first Premier on the granting of responsible government in WA - a position that went to his friend John (later Lord) Forrest. Brown died in 1905, aged 61.

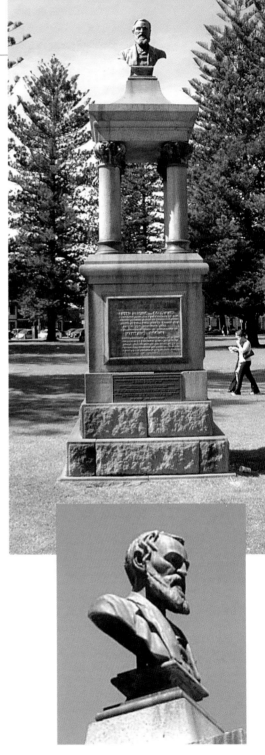

In 1912 Kimberley pioneer George Julius Brockman, commissioned well-known Fremantle sculptor Pietro Porcelli, to make the memorial. The 2.5m-high structure was originally intended for Broome but Brockman was persuaded that it should be erected in Fremantle where more people could see it.

The memorial was unveiled at a public ceremony in 1913 by Lady Forrest, nee Margaret Hamersley, who had once been engaged to Brown. The engagement had ended when Brown volunteered to head the expedition to find Panter, Harding and Goldwyer.

And so it remained, largely forgotten and ignored until 1988 when a group of Murdoch University academics began moves to have the Aborigines killed at La Grange acknowledged on the memorial. In 1990 Brown's head was chiselled off. According to a newspaper report this was thought to be "a protest against the public recognition of a man with a reputation for mistreating Aborigines."

A replacement bust was installed and the original head secretly returned in 1993. In 1994 another plaque was added to commemorate the La Grange Aboriginal victims and "all Aboriginal people who died during the invasion of their country". In 1995 this too was stolen, but reinstalled in 1996.

FOOTNOTE: Maitland Brown's older brother Kenneth, the father of Edith Cowan, was hung in old Perth Gaol in June 1876 for the murder of his second wife, Mary Anne, Edith's stepmother, in Geraldton five months earlier. Three trials were needed before he was convicted and providing legal costs for the defence proved a huge financial burden for Maitland Brown.

# When a watering-hole was a benchmark for job-seekers

Esplanade Hotel
Corner of Collie Street and Marine Terrace
Map Ref: 12

**I**n the 1940s when times were tough, Fremantle's Esplanade Hotel became an unofficial employment centre for men seeking work.

They would sit on wooden benches at the front of Marine Terrace and hope to pick up work on the waterfront from employers needing casual labour.

The so-called Paddy Troy benches are still there today, squarely built and solid, positioned against the hotel's front wall at one end of the long verandah, clearly visible from the former Trades Hall building on the other side of Collie Street where Troy had his office. They are both a testament to the times and a tribute to the man, Patrick Laurence Troy, a folk hero among waterside workers.

*Patrick Laurence Troy*

The Paddy Troy influence before and during the Depression, and for many years after, was wide and powerful. As the communist secretary of the Maritime Workers' Union for 25 years, Troy played a significant role in the growing power of the union movement and the realisation of his dream to establish a central body for WA unions, the Trades and Labor Council.

It was his idea to place benches on the hotel verandah to give the unemployed some semblance of dignity. Until then, such job seekers had to sit around the street gutters opposite in the hope of being offered some casual work.

The seats, which were twice removed and subsequently restored on protest, are a microcosm of the chameleon nature of the hotel. Of any building in Fremantle, the Esplanade has possibly best mirrored the changing needs of the community during the past century.

Thus it has variously changed its colours from a family hotel providing all the niceties for a seaside holiday to a daily watering-hole for beer-thirsty workers (at one point complete with gymnasium and boxing ring). Today, of course, its reputation is of a large, world-class facility which accommodates visitors from around the globe.

In retrospect, the use of the hotel site as a people's place began well before the Esplanade was built in 1895. Forty five years earlier, when the first convicts arrived in the colony aboard *Scindian*, there was nowhere to accommodate them. So it was agreed to lease two wool stores on Lots 150 and 152 on the corner of Marine Terrace from its influential owner, Captain Daniel Scott. This served as temporary accommodation until the Imperial Convict Establishment, later Fremantle Prison, was built.

Over the years, there have been many owners of the hotel, ranging from

individuals to corporate identities, including the local Swan Brewery. Its changing complexion took a major leap in the immediate build-up to the defence of the America's Cup in 1987, when the-then owners - Winterbottom Holdings - invested $14 million to renovate and expand facilities in anticipation of Fremantle's reborn status as a city of unique interest and attraction. As recent history and a subsequent tourism boom show, it was a sound investment in Fremantle's new future.

Since 1991 under the new ownership of Camellia Holdings, the Esplanade Hotel has been further expanded to provide more first-class accommodation for the huge influx of national and international visitors. Some $34 million has been spent to upgrade and extend guest accommodation, as well as add resort-style recreational and conference facilities.

Inevitably, this has brought many necessary changes to the building of pre-America's Cup days. What has not changed, however, is the unique appearance of a hotel surrounded by a street-level verandah, a much admired and elegant feature of earlier times . . .

. . . and, of course, the Paddy Troy benches.

FOOTNOTE: Paddy Troy was educated at Christian Brothers College, Fremantle. He left the Labor Party and joined the Communist Party after disagreeing with Labor's economic policies during the Depression. In 1940, during the Menzies Government, he was jailed for three months for possessing printed material which had been made illegal. He died in 1978, aged 70.

*The Esplanade Hotel at the beginning of the 20th Century, an assembly point for processions and pageants.*

*The Paddy Troy benches.*

# Fighting prelude to a showcase Strip

Cappuccino Strip
South Terrace
Map Ref: 13

**V**isitors enjoying the carefree, cosmopolitan vibes of Fremantle's Cappuccino Strip might be surprised to learn that not so long ago it was a place where you would never walk alone, especially after dark. Indeed, the precise spot which later generated the spread of pavement tables and chairs beneath their colorful canopy of umbrellas was one of the not-so-nice places to be.

At the corner of Collie Street and South Terrace, Papa Luigi's Pizza and Coffee Lounge attracted working men, mostly local Italians, during the day and, after six o'clock, groups of young hoodlums. The site of Clegg's Furniture store many years before, the corner venue had been essentially an amusement parlour since the mid-1960s. The coffee lounge took up about a quarter of the area at the front of the premises, beyond which was a much larger room with pool tables and pinball machines. A flight of wooden steps beneath a trapdoor led to a basement where men would meet to play cards and make small bets on the outcome.

One day in 1977, the new owner of Papa Luigi's, Nunzio Gumina, heard on the grapevine that a gang of youths from Coolbellup planned to come to the café that night to fight the local Fremantle gang, the former always identifiable by their black T-shirts. Nunzio, who had been night manager of the café since its inception, was well aware what this might mean to his new business. "It was a tough town and a dangerous place in those days," he said. "Shortly after I bought Papa Luigi's I had been warned by the council to clean it up or they would shut me down. When I heard about the fight I had already been getting through to some of these kids with help from a welfare group. Having grown up in Fremantle, I also knew many of their parents. But there were so many young hoods who didn't take any notice of anyone, police included. Anyone was a target for a bashing or mugging. People were just too scared to walk alone on this side of the street."

What happened that night is still a bit hazy. "Somehow I managed to stop the fight happening," Nunzio recalled. "I went out into the street and met them and said: 'If you guys want to fight, come back tomorrow night and

*South Terrace, December 1918, with a naval procession heading towards Market Street.*

*Where it all began... the site of the original Papa Luigi's in 1905, when it was Clegg's Furniture Store. The building is also clearly visible in the recent colour photograph above.*

we'll do it officially.' After a bit more talk, they accepted that and went away. What I had in mind was setting up a boxing match between the Coolbellup and Fremantle boys, so they could settle their differences that way without destroying my property."

Which was exactly what happened - in the basement below Papa Luigi's where four pillars roughly formed the shape and size of a boxing ring. With help from the welfare group, a mat and boxing gloves were borrowed from the local YMCA. Enough rope to encircle the four pillars was donated by the North Fremantle Rope and Twine Company. Nunzio bought boxing medallions and a trophy from a local shop. That night some 100 youths queued up through Papa Luigi's to make their way through the trapdoor to the basement below, where the fights began - three two-minute rounds each - and differences were settled. As Nunzio recalled: "At the end of it we presented them with their medallions. The trophy winner was a little Italian guy who flattened a big fellow from Coolbellup. They hugged one another and went home and we never had any more problems after that."

Two years later, Nunzio's entrepreneurial initiative came to the fore again with an approach to the Fremantle City Council to redevelop the amusement parlour. One of his regulars, an architect who had been to Italy, offered to draw up a plan to create an Italian piazza-style café. "It had always been my dream," said Nunzio. There was resistance at first and, only months after submitting the plan, was it given a three-month trial. Tables and chairs and umbrellas went out onto South Terrace for the first time and Papa Luigi's Café, thus renamed when it went alfresco, became the catalyst for the early beginnings of the Cappuccino Strip.

Huge changes followed in the ensuing years leading up to and following the America's Cup defence in 1987. With the turn of the century, the Strip has continued to reinvent itself many times. Names have changed and come and gone, the streetscape has seen numerous trials and tribulations, but at the end of the day - and night - South Terrace has made a veritable by-the-sea-change to become one of the most popular, busy and safe streets in Western Australia.

# America's Cup gave drinking a new flavour

Sail & Anchor, Norfolk and Newport hotels
South Terrace
Map Ref: 13

**A**s well as being central to Fremantle's markets and the Cappuccino Strip, the Sail & Anchor holds a special place in a unique environment as Fremantle's most visited hotel.

Originally the Freemason's Hotel and Tavern, its existence as a hotel dates back to 1856, although it was largely rebuilt to its current structure in 1903. However, it wasn't until 1985, when the place was refurbished and given its present name in preparation for the 1987 America's Cup defence that it took on an extraordinary new lease of life. Today that interprets into thousands of visitors a week to possibly the best known location in Fremantle on the corner of Henderson Street and South Terrace.

Almost any day when it's not raining, it is a visible source of conviviality and fun, with people sitting at crowded tables on the Henderson Street walkway lapping up the sights and sustenance of their choice. On a hot day, the beer flows outside and inside the front bar and beyond, hand-pumped from kegs in the cellar below, the way it always was in the best English pub tradition. Behind the hotel's mission statement - *to make the world a more sociable place, one beer at a time* - lies an unprecedented success story which had its beginnings at this, Australia's first micro-brewery. It began with a small group of interested people getting together with the aim of producing a "beer with a difference" and grew rapidly with the ultimate establishment of the Matilda Bay Brewing Company, now selling its brews nationwide.

While the hotel and that company have since gone their separate ways, the Sail & Anchor continues to produce its exclusive brands of draught beer - among them House Lager, Indian Pale Ale, Dockers Wheat Beer, Brass Monkey Stout and ESB (Extra Special Bitter). It also has on tap brands which emerged from the subsequent expansion of the Matilda Bay company, such as Redback, the multi-award-winning wheat beer, and Dogbolter Special Dark Lager, which gained its name from the original strong ale brewed and served at the Sail & Anchor during the America's Cup.

Two other hotels, the Norfolk and the Newport, also have special identities in the Cappuccino Strip. The Norfolk underwent a major reconstruction and renaming in 1986, just a year short of its centenary as the Oddfellows Hotel, then a much larger and very different looking building. Verandahs that encroached above and onto the footpath of South Terrace and Norfolk Street were removed and about a third of the building demolished to make way for a leisurely, shaded courtyard - in direct contrast to the noisier, crowded bar setting of the previous establishment. An earlier newspaper article headed "Revolutionary new hotel plan," described how the planners wanted to achieve a family environment with "no louts, pop, din or stubbies." There would be no slot machines, video games or pool tables at the Norfolk.

Meanwhile, at the other end of the crowded South Terrace, the former Newcastle Club Tavern was about to undergo similar transformation. The run-

down 1897 building had more than $200,000 of building and court orders hanging over it and faced a very bleak future. However, all this changed when the new lessee decided to embark on an exhaustive restoration programme which took five months and more than $500,000 to complete, including the reinstatement of a two-storey verandah which was a copy of the cast-iron original. The restored building, now appropriately renamed the Newport Hotel after the city where Australia had wrested the America's Cup three years earlier, was officially reopened on a Friday night in October 1986. The rest of the weekend the hotel was jammed with thousands of people streaming through to witness the reincarnation.

*Top: The front bar of the Sail & Anchor, where beer is hand-pumped from below.*

*Centre: The Norfolk Hotel, given a new look and lease of life in 1986.*

*Bottom: The Newport, formerly the Newcastle Club Hotel, restored and rescued from a bleak future.*

# Markets that offer lifestyle bargains

Fremantle Markets
Corner of South Terrace and Henderson Street
Map Ref: 14

**J**ust a few years ago, a young man sporting dreadlocks and jeans would take his place in an allotted area in the fruit and vegetable section of the Fremantle Markets and make music on his guitar.

An open guitar case next to him would occasionally clatter noisily as a coin was tossed in. Some people would stop, look, listen and then move on. Others just walked by, avoiding eye contact with the young performer. Just another busker trying to make good.

Fremantle Markets has seen plenty of free entertainers over the years - singers, sword swallowers, magicians, violinists, poets and story-tellers. Even a man dressed up as a cat. Most of them, like the passing parade of onlookers, have moved on, never to be heard or seen again.

But this one was different. His name was John Butler, a young man on a musical mission. What people may have thought of his presence or his performance didn't matter one way or another. His concern was to be a successful writer and player of music.

In retrospect, it didn't take him long to get there. Just eight years on, he was scaling the heights of Australian rock music as leader of the John Butler Trio. The independent band became a phenomenon of the times, making music history with albums like *Three*, which quickly sold more than 100,000 copies and *Sunrise Over Sea*, the first independently produced and distributed studio album to top the Australian chart on release.

John Butler's connection with Fremantle Markets is synonymous with never knowing quite what to expect at one of Fremantle's most popular landmarks. Therein also lies one of its great charms.

Indeed, its earlier history as Western Australia's first wholesale fruit and vegetable market almost dulls by comparison with its later life, resuscitated and re-launched in 1975 as a general market, but still enshrined within its original limestone walls and atmosphere.

The markets were seen as a major boost for Fremantle when the Premier, Sir John Forrest laid the foundation stone in November 1897. By mid-1898 a caretaker had been appointed and sales were soon flourishing, as noted in The Morning Herald's market report one December morning, scantily describing the available vegetables as "good and of varied assortment."

The wholesale price of a dozen bunches of mint, parsley or radishes was sixpence, or just five cents. A gallon of beans cost two cents, peas five cents or a hundredweight (cwt) of potatoes or onions the equivalent of $1. Eggs, however, must have been a luxury item, because the price was 1/6d, or 15 cents a dozen.

Market gardeners came from the outlying areas of Coogee and Spearwood and as far south as Mandurah to sell their fruit and vegetables. Some arrived at 3 o'clock in the morning and had to wait three hours before they could unload their goods.

By the 1920s, however, hard times were falling on the markets, partly caused by the establishment of the Central Perth Markets where growers now directed their business. Trading in Fremantle closed soon after and the buildings, gradually falling into disrepair, were used only for warehousing.

The renaissance of Fremantle Markets came in 1975 when a private development company leased the complex and renovated the old buildings. A plan to implement trading similar to the markets

in Europe and Asia, with more than 150 individual stores selling anything and everything to tempt the appetites of casual shoppers, was immediately successful - and has been so ever since.

Today, more than 30,000 people on average visit the markets each weekend, the numbers boosted further on public holidays. They come from all over the world, individually and on organised tours. And they come from WA, locals who know that this is a place where they can find cosmopolitan life and entertainment as well as something interesting or unusual to buy. The vegetables and fruit maintain their place as an enduring part of the markets, and the late-afternoon auctions towards the end of trade offer entertainment as well as fresh bargains.

You won't find John Butler there any more, unless one day he decides to make a return appearance. Meanwhile, Fremantle has fast established a reputation as a leading Australian centre of contemporary music.

# Living the cottage life with conviction

Warders' Cottages
Henderson Street
Map Ref: 15

**T**he neat row of cottages with their stone walls and smart frontages facing Henderson Street provides a glimpse of the living standards of prison warders and their families in the immediate years after they were built in the early 1850s.

It can, however, be little more than a glimpse. The cottages were built by convicts hurriedly and as a matter of necessity to meet the extreme demands of the time. They were basic buildings with basic amenities. There were no verandahs then and no garden walls. There was little emphasis on serving the individual needs of the warders' families but, rather, the urgent need to provide somewhere to shelter as they, along with the convicts, were arriving in shiploads from England.

Consequently, privacy had to give way to a generally shared existence. Two families were allocated the six-room home, which often meant there were as many as 10 children in each cottage. The niceties of life necessarily took second place to the essentials, like cooking and washing and getting fresh water from the well. Residents shared the workload as well as the produce of extensive vegetable gardens at the front of, as well as behind the cottages. These were all part of the communal life. Indeed, it was not until 50 years later, when extra flights of stairs were installed, that people living upstairs no longer had to walk through the downstairs neighbours' rooms to reach their own space.

It is not hard to imagine the friction and the tension these conditions would have provoked. For the warder coming home after a hard day at the prison, the strain at times must have been near-intolerable.

The warder's job at hand and the prospect of a better future were the reason for being there in the first place. But the experience of George Bartlett, a warder who arrived in Fremantle aboard *Palestine* in January 1863, gives some idea of how tough it

*The flogging triangle (reconstructed) where prisoners were punished.*

could be. Bartlett was a painter by trade who had served in the Royal Engineers and been a warder at London's Chatham Prison. He and his pregnant wife Mary, along with their three-year-old twin sons, most likely spent their first year in one of the cottages before he was shifted to manage convict painters at Perth Gaol. That was early in 1864. A little more than two years later, in August 1866, he and his family returned to Fremantle where the warder was put in charge of a chain gang. On the last day of that month Bartlett was brutally assaulted by a prisoner, inflicting serious internal injuries. The warder recovered from the beating but died of

a heart attack just 11 months later which, a doctor assessed, had been induced by the earlier injuries. Bartlett had been well regarded by his seniors and his widow was subsequently granted five shillings a week (50c) from the Imperial Compensation Fund on the recommendation of the Governor. Given that her husband's wages had been £25 ($50) a year plus accommodation - and that there were no social benefits in those days - it was probably a reasonable amount to receive.

There are many stories of Fremantle warders and their experiences, often harsh ones. Prisoner assaults on warders were not uncommon and often were punished by floggings in the prison yard. Typical was a case in 1893 when a Chinese prisoner attacked a chief warder with an eating utensil, causing painful head injuries. The prisoner was sentenced to three dozen lashes. Unlike the prison, there are few stories about early life in the cottages, which were built almost out of desperation by Edmund Henderson seven years before the prison itself was completed in 1859 (although the main cell block was half finished and began taking convicts in 1855). As Comptroller General of Convicts, Henderson had to achieve a difficult balance based on an unpredictable human supply from the UK and resultant demand in Fremantle. In 1860, for example, just one convict - a military man from Bermuda - arrived in Western Australia.

The later years are better documented and, indeed, after the turn of the century life improved dramatically. Facilities were changed and introduced to bring privacy for families. The outside kitchen, scullery and wash house, formerly shared by four families, were replaced by individual facilities inside each cottage. In 1906 the additional stairs were installed.

Indeed, by the 1930s, despite the hard times of the Great Depression, life at the warders' cottages was almost idyllic by comparison. According to one descendant's account, the childhood years at No 17 Henderson Street were full of fun and neighbourly friendship. The premises remained small, but cosy. Perhaps the only drawback was use of the privy on a cold night, still a solitary Australian icon, at the back of the garden. At least by then it was no longer shared by others.

With the closure of Fremantle Prison in 1991, the warders' cottages were renovated as State housing properties, carefully restored to maintain their original design, materials and structure. Their tenants are no longer prison warders, but their view from the back verandah - Fremantle Prison - is much the same, and certainly a reminder of those who were there before.

# Town Hall celebrations went off with a bang

Fremantle Town Hall
Kings Square
Map Ref: 16

**J**une 22, 1887 was a very special Wednesday for the people of Fremantle, marking two significant events - Queen Victoria's Golden Jubilee and, perhaps of even greater interest to locals, the official opening of the Fremantle Town Hall.

It had taken more than a decade to reach this important milestone in Fremantle's young history. It would take less than 48 hours after the opening ceremony for the occasion to acquire a tragic epitaph.

The Governor, Sir Frederick Napier Broome, officiated at the launch on the Wednesday, after which followed a sports carnival and, later that evening, a ball in the splendid new auditorium. The festivities resumed the next day, ending with a children's fancy dress ball. All proceeded as planned until after the ball had ended when, soon after midnight, the unexpected and terrible event occurred. A man walked into the town hall, sought out a town councillor, produced a revolver - and shot him in the neck.

The victim of this assault was 69-year-old John Snook, a well regarded member of the community who had come from England with his wife in 1853. Curiously, his attacker was William Conroy, the landlord of the nearby National Hotel in High Street, who was well known to several councillors, including the mayor.

Maybe the extraordinary event would not have been so horrific had Snook survived the attack. Tragically, the councillor died three months after the shooting and the charges against Conroy were upgraded from shooting with intent to murder to wilful murder.

In the subsequent Supreme Court case it was officially revealed that Conroy had gone to the Town Hall earlier on the night of June 23, hoping to gain entry to the official function. However, he had been refused by Cr Snook, partly it was believed because the publican was inebriated. Later Conroy admitted killing Snook but claimed he had been "of unsound mind" at the time and not responsible for his actions.

The judge was not convinced and in addressing Conroy before sentence, said: "This poor fellow who was your victim was shot down by you for some reason or another which you say was because he would not let you into a room where some entertainment was going on. You watched for your victim and you shot him dead. You gave as your reason for doing it - 'He turned me out; so now I have turned him out'."

The jury found Conroy guilty and he was sentenced to death, becoming the last person to be hanged at Perth Gaol -

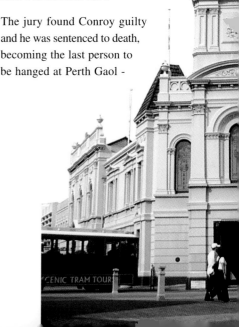

*The 1920s look... eight girls dressed as shepherdesses parade at a fancy dress ball.*

*A huge crowd gathers outside the Town Hall for the launch of the Fremantle Tramways in November 1905. The balcony, used for official functions, was removed in 1927.*

on November 18 that year, barely five months after the shooting.

Despite its inauspicious beginnings, the Town Hall quickly went from strength to strength as the administrative headquarters and social focal point of the city. It had taken 11 years to establish since public land in South Terrace had been set aside for that purpose.

However, it was soon determined a more central location was needed, the Kings Square site being made available by the church's trustees.

triangular-shaped building with its tall spire and specially imported English clock

quickly became a landmark, audible and visible from all approaches, as it is still today. Its spacious central hall became the centre for a huge variety of events and entertainment ranging from concerts to community singing, music hall variety, stage plays, religious celebrations, bands, balls, film shows and public meetings.

Despite renovations and additions over the years, such as the Civic and Administration Building and Exhibition Hall during the 1960s, the Town Hall has managed to hang on to its essential, original character - described by the National Trust of Australia as being in "the tradition of renaissance European civic design." A major restoration in 1985 spruced it up without detracting from its former glory.

Indeed, when two years later Fremantle once again embarked on festivities to mark the Town Hall's centenary, the clock was turned back to include similar celebrations of 100 years before, including a street fair, a gala ball and a children's fancy dress party . . .

. . . and, of course, a re-enactment of the fatal shooting .

# The day a wharf dispute erupted into Bloody Sunday

The Thomas Edwards Memorial Fountain
Kings Square
Map Ref: 17

**T**he nondescript and faded fountain on the Adelaide Street side of Kings Square is a reminder of a little known but violent episode in Western Australia's industrial history.

It honours the memory of Thomas Edwards, a lumper (waterside worker) and largely forgotten labour martyr, who died as a result of a fractured skull he received during The Battle of the Barricades between Fremantle waterside workers and armed police on Victoria Quay on what became known as Bloody Sunday, May 4, 1919.

Edwards, born in Victoria, joined the Lumpers' Union at Fremantle in 1917, just months before a nation-wide wharf strike which led to the Commonwealth Government calling in volunteers - National Workers - and giving them an undertaking of permanent employment. With no dole, and little or no work, unionists like Edwards struggled to support their families.

In January, 1919, an outbreak in the Eastern States of a particularly severe strain of influenza led to WA being virtually isolated, resulting in an acute shortage of imported food.

On April 17, 1919, Hal Colebatch had become leader of the National Party and Premier following the resignation of Sir Henry Lefroy. While he was involved in political manoeuvreings, including trying to secure a lower house seat in State Parliament, the wharf crisis erupted. By the end of April the food situation in WA had become serious and there was huge pressure on the Government to unload the recently arrived SS Dimboola which was carrying a considerable quantity of perishable goods. Before this could happen it was considered necessary to erect barricades on the wharf to keep demonstrating lumpers at bay while unloading was carried out by National Workers.

Colebatch accepted an offer from the cargo consignees to do the job themselves and it was secretly decided that the barricades be erected on the overcast morning of Sunday, May 4. But it was a badly-kept secret. When the volunteer workmen, accompanied by the Premier, travelling downriver from Perth in two launches, reached the Fremantle railway and traffic bridges they were greeted by a big contingent of demonstrators. Perched atop the bridges they rained large stones and scrap iron onto the passing launches. Fortunately, there were only minor injuries to some on board.

When the launch party and other volunteers reached the wharf a squad of mounted and foot police, armed with batons, succeeded in pushing back a crowd of lumpers, armed with shovels, pickhandles, stones and a variety of other missiles. The arrival of another 700 men from the bridges and Fremantle swelled the crowd, including women and children, to about 4000 and the situation became ugly.

A number of police were injured by the missiles thrown at them. They were then ordered to fix bayonets. One of the lumpers, Edward "Knockabout" Brown, walking unarmed towards the waterfront, was bayoneted in the thigh by police. The president of the Lumpers' Union, William Renton, called on his group to rescue him. Renton was then knocked down by a police baton, causing head injuries. The 41-year-old Edwards, going to the aid of Renton, was struck on the head by a police baton or rifle butt and collapsed.

The situation deteriorated. Shots were fired toward the police from the crowd, the Riot Act was read by a Justice of the Peace and police firearms loaded. At this critical moment the officer-in-charge of the Fremantle police district, Inspector William Sellenger, stepped forward and defused the situation. At a later hurried conference between Colebatch, the Police Commissioner and union officials it was agreed that the barricades-erecting party could withdraw without further interference. The police also withdrew. Colebatch and his party negotiated a safe passage for their return journey to Perth.

Their departure was greeted with mingled cheering and hooting and the crowd slowly dispersed. Later, a group of lumpers returned and threw the barricades into the harbour.

Edwards, one of more than 30 lumpers and policemen injured in the struggle, had been taken to Fremantle Hospital where he died three days later, immediately being elevated to the status of union hero and martyr. His funeral on May 9 brought Fremantle and other parts of the State to a standstill. More than 5000 people, including John Curtin, later wartime Prime Minister, marched in the funeral procession which was headed by Renton - on horseback with his head still bandaged.

*Above: Day of the funeral, when a huge crowd lined up to pay their last respects to Thomas Edwards (left)*

The jury at the Edwards inquest returned a verdict of accidental death, unable to determine who had fractured his skull. The Government awarded a $1,372 pension to his family and the union movement conducted an appeal which provided a shop and home in Fremantle for Mrs Edwards and her daughters aged 14, six and 18 months.

The repercussions of The Battle of the Barricades were substantial. The National Workers withdrew permanently from the waterfront. Colebatch's position as Premier was badly damaged. In ill health and unable to find a seat in the Legislative Assembly, he resigned eight days after Edwards' funeral. His Government had lasted exactly one month - the shortest term in office in WA history. Colebatch continued as a Minister in the subsequent Mitchell Government. He later became WA's Agent-General in London and represented WA in the Senate. He was knighted in1927 and died in 1953.

Sarah Jane Edwards, who had been on the wharf the day her husband was injured and later shielded her dying husband from the sun as he lay on the grass with the other casualties outside hospital waiting for treatment, remained bitter about the events of May 4. She remarried about 20 years later and died in March, 1964, aged. 80.

The Edwards memorial by Fremantle scupltor Pietro Porcellli, in rustic granite with a marble plaque, was unveiled in 1919 by Renton and stood outside the Trades Hall in Collie Street until the building was sold in 1968. It was then stored at the rear of the Waterside Workers Federation office before being restored and relocated to Kings Square in 1982.

# Italian sculptor's lasting legacy

Pietro Porcelli Sculpture
Kings Square
Map Ref: 18

**The death of** Italian-born Pietro Porcelli, often described as "the well-known Fremantle sculptor", in Perth in 1943 at the age of 71 went virtually unremarked.

By then Porcelli, who had spent 62 years in Australia, had fallen on hard times. A virtual recluse, he was largely forgotten. Yet his work in Western Australia, particularly in Fremantle, not only endures but is still universally admired.

The statue of C.Y. O'Connor on Victoria Quay is generally regarded as his greatest achievement. However, he was also responsible for the Maitland Brown Memorial, the Marmion Memorial (an ornate celtic cross under Fremantle's Proclamation Tree), the Alexander Forrest Monument in Perth, the Piesse Monument in Katanning, numerous war memorials throughout WA, the busts of prominent early WA leaders and the Peace statue in Midland.

Porcelli was born in the small town of Bisceglie, near Bari, a coastal city on the Adriatic. When he was eight his father Leonardo left for Australia, taking Pietro with him but leaving his mother and sister behind. They settled originally in New South Wales. Pietro's artistic abilities were recognised early and he was instructed at the NSW Academy of Art in Sydney until his father sent him to Naples to study at the Royal Academy.

He obtained a diploma of the Academy and won gold and silver medals in Italy for his work. Back in Sydney at the age of 26, Porcelli found life hard in difficult economic times. The discovery of gold in WA and the promise of a more prosperous life proved irresistable. He and his father arrived in Fremantle in August 1898 and settled in Henry Street.

Leonardo went into business as an importer of Italian goods with a store in Pakenham Street and his talented son quickly established his presence as a sculptor. His first work, a life-size bust of the Premier, Sir John Forrest - the first to be made of a WA citizen and the first by a local artist - was completed in December 1898. It was later purchased by the Forrest family and now has pride of place in the foyer of Parliament House in Perth.

The memorial to William Marmion, a prominent Fremantle citizen and a Minister in Forrest's Government, unveiled in early 1902, was Porcelli's first major work and brought him to public attention. Although other major work soon followed, financial problems were never far away during Porcelli's life. In 1907, swept up in the gold boom, he went prospecting. But the attempt to strike it rich was short-lived and unsuccessful. He was soon back in Fremantle "determined to stick to art."

His design for the O'Connor statue (far right) was chosen from 17 submissions. With the security afforded by the $3,000 commission, Porcelli married Welsh governess Martha Goodwin in Fremantle in 1910. A daughter was born that year and a son the following year. The family's first home in Pakenham Street was very close to the old stone-walled store in Marine Terrace that Porcelli used as a studio.

The statue was described as "Signor Porcelli's masterpiece" and was said to be good enough to endure for a thousand years. The honorary architect said that the committee had received a bargain ... "more value for their money in this memorial than in any other similar work in Christendom."

After the unveiling of the Maitland Brown memorial in 1913 Porcelli's reputation and financial position were at an all-time high. But it didn't last. By 1915 he had entered another period of financial hardship compounded by ill-health and had moved from Fremantle. After World War I he was busy with war memorials and his last public work in WA was the Midland Railways Workshops Peace statue, unveiled in 1925.

Porcelli suffered a major disappointment when he and other local artists were not considered good enough to do the Kings Park memorial to Lord

Forrest who had been one of Porcelli's biggest supporters. He relocated to Melbourne where he worked on the Shrine of Remembrance. However, his attempt at a new life received a major setback when he was hit by a car and knocked under a tram in the city.

He returned to WA soon after. Despite further illness and the collapse of his marriage he continued working and was remembered at his boarding house as a retiring figure who continued shaping clay until the end.

In the 1980s the Italian community decided to recognise Porcelli's achievements. Fremantle sculptor Greg James was commissioned by the Italian Club, with money raised by local Italians, to do the $22,500 life-like sculpture (left). It was unveiled in 1993.

# Some interesting signs of the times

BELOW: The colourful brick-line which skirts the paths and buildings of the West End of Fremantle was once the very edge of the Indian Ocean. Boats were rowed ashore to deliver goods from the ships, the cargo often hoisted to the safety of dry lofts in warehouses on the water's edge, such as those beneath the roofline of the Bateman buildings in Croke Street.

ABOVE: The circular sandstone plinth near Fremantle Bridge just across the river in Beach Street often goes unnoticed. Once it was very central to Fremantle's transport needs, housing the winch that hauled barges from the river bank opposite.

RIGHT: The horse trough in Phillimore Street has been preserved in its original form as a reminder of when times - and transport - were very different. Horses and stables were an integral part of Fremantle life and trade during the goldrush years. There were also road signs for drivers - and penalties for speedsters!

How times change . . The Municipal Tramways building in High Street when tramlines were being laid in 1905 (above) and the same building today with its showrooms and café.

*RIGHT: Culley's Tea Rooms in High Street are the last, wholly family owned business (fourth generation) still trading in Fremantle. It was founded in 1925 by Ted Culley, who came from England to WA as a 15-year-old, worked in the goldfields and then made enough money to launch the tea rooms with his wife Alice. The tea rooms still operate along traditional lines, with all the bread and cakes baked on the premises and served fresh daily. Each day as many as 1200 tourists and local people visit what has become a Fremantle institution.*

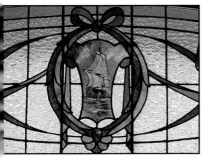

*LEFT: Above the main entrance to the Fremantle Chamber of Commerce in Phillimore Street is a glass window which, on closer inspection, bears an image of Lord Nelson's famous flagship, Victory, in which he died while defeating the French and Spanish at the battle of Trafalgar. The Fremantle connection is through Captain Charles Fremantle's father, Thomas, who as captain of Neptune, fought alongside Nelson and was one of the great heroes of the historic sea battle.*

*RIGHT: Unlike all the other buildings and shops in High Street, the TAB Office is set back noticeably from the pavement. The reason is simple. When it was built in the 1970s, State Planning Policy plans were to widen High Street in conjunction with the building of a new coastal freeway along the alignment of Cliff Street, which would have meant demolishing shop fronts on one side of the road. This did not go ahead. Neither did a move in 1999 to put a two-storey façade on the building in the same style as there originally. Ironically, the TAB office has been left behind, rather than ahead of the times.*

*LEFT: Visitors to the South Mole may wonder for what purpose these rusty capstans and wheels were used. The answer is simple-they were part of Western Australia's defence system during World War II, and all that remain of what was once an anti-submarine net which stretched across to the North Mole to prevent enemy submarines from entering Inner Harbour.*

# George King, a man for all seasons

**I**n the display cabinet in St John's Church, Fremantle, the portrait of George King stands out among the collection of old photographs and drawings depicting the church's early history. It shows the strong, intelligent, bearded face of a man on a mission. Indeed, the Reverend George King was very much a pioneer in his own right in the early days of the Swan River Colony. Physically and mentally, he was tough. One imagines that had he not been a man of the cloth, he would have been a leader of men in other ways.

As it was, King came to Western Australia after the Archbishop of Canterbury had been asked to send someone to establish a more permanent Church of England presence in Fremantle. Until he arrived in 1841, the citizens of Fremantle had to depend on fortnightly visits from the Perth-based Colonial Chaplain who would hold services at the small courthouse next to the Round House. However, these visits ended abruptly when locals refused to continue paying the chaplain's travel expenses, thus leaving Fremantle people without a minister, let alone a church.

George King soon changed all that. Born in County Tyrone, the son of an Irish linen merchant, he moved rapidly from acquiring an arts degree in Dublin in 1836 to ordainment in 1837, marriage two years later and migration to Western Australia in 1841 as a missionary for the Society for the Propagation of the Gospel. Then aged 28, he arrived aboard *Ganges* with his wife and two small children.

It seems life continued fast and full for the Kings. Under his direction, within two years the original St John's Church (bottom left) was built, occupying the area now outlined and marked by a plaque in the centre of Kings Square. In the same period, he established two other churches, one in Mandurah and the other in Pinjarra. In addition - and without any substantial assistance from colonial authorities - he and his wife set up a school for Aboriginal children locally.

His energy and enthusiasm were matched by the many tasks he accomplished and, not least, the sheer size of his parish. In an 1846 report to his seniors in London, King describes his extended diocese as "900 square miles", administering to the needs of settlers in the Canning and Murray river areas, as well as those in Fremantle, Mandurah and Pinjarra. He must have been a man of extraordinary energy and fitness. Apart from morning and evening services and sermons every Sunday at St John's and at the gaol, he rode horseback to all these far-flung places every month, sometimes battling floods and storms, or extreme heat to reach his parishioners. There is no record of where he actually lived in Fremantle, although in a report he says he "resides within half a mile of the town." It is suggested King Street in East Fremantle may have been named after him.

Ultimately, his work took its toll. In 1846 his health began to deteriorate and, in January 1849, he and his family moved to NSW. In Sydney, King began a long relationship with St Andrew's Cathedral and its parish, a move which eventually turned sour over church constitutional disagreements in which he became entangled.

From 1863 he moved progressively from one parish appointment to another, always involved in special interests. Among these, he was a founder and sometimes president of the NSW Institution for the Deaf and Dumb and a director for the Society for the Relief of Destitute Children. He died at Homebush in 1899, his wife following a year later. They were survived by two daughters and a son.

Meanwhile, King had outlived the church he built in Fremantle, which increasingly became inadequate for the growing Fremantle congregation. A decision to demolish it made way for St John's as it is now, a splendid blend of early English and Gothic styles of architecture, consecrated in 1882. The agreement with civic authorities to locate the church on the northern side of the square allowed the extension of High Street through its centre, as well as space for a future town hall. This arrangement also helped finance the building of the new church, to which the bell tower and a large vestry were added in 1907 and 1922 respectively.

The church grounds were fenced off until the 1960s, when the City Council began a restoration project with the closure of High Street through the square. The first enclosure, a high picket fence, was replaced in the early 1920s by a lower chain fence - but not in time to prevent the locals involved removing pickets to use as weapons in the Fremantle wharf riots of 1919.

# The blacksmith's son who became a hero

Sir Hughie Edwards Memorial
Kings Square
Map Ref: 20

**H**ughie Edwards is one of Fremantle's famous sons. He was Australia's most decorated serviceman and the first airman to be awarded a Victoria Cross in World War II.

The bronze statue in Kings Square provides an immediate insight into Edwards' fame - a helmeted airman looking skywards to the challenges ahead. In fact, he was not always the best of pilots, crashing at least two aircraft which almost cost him his life.

Edwards' determination, however, was unquestionable. It got him through a flight-path of life whereby he rose from shipping clerk to war hero, air commodore, a knight of the realm and Governor of Western Australia - Sir Hughie Edwards, VC KCMG DSO OBE DFC.

In other circumstances, Hughie Idwal Edwards might well have gone on to fame as an Australian Rules footballer. He played several games for South Fremantle and was invited to try out for Essendon. He also played grade cricket. But first the Depression, then the war intervened, and thus began an air force career that lasted 28 years - from air cadet with the RAAF at Point Cook in 1935, to Air Commodore with the RAF in 1963.

Of Welsh descent, Edwards was one of a family of five children. His father was a blacksmith who, with his wife and one child, had moved to WA from Wales in 1909 seeking a new life in the land of opportunity. They had a small home in White Gum Valley where Edwards was born in 1914. He and his two brothers attended the primary school there, before starting secondary education at Fremantle

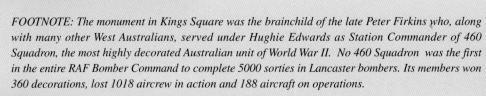

*FOOTNOTE: The monument in Kings Square was the brainchild of the late Peter Firkins who, along with many other West Australians, served under Hughie Edwards as Station Commander of 460 Squadron, the most highly decorated Australian unit of World War II. No 460 Squadron was the first in the entire RAF Bomber Command to complete 5000 sorties in Lancaster bombers. Its members won 360 decorations, lost 1018 aircrew in action and 188 aircraft on operations.*

Boys School. He left school at 14 to help support his family.

Life really opened up for young Hughie in 1935 when, after a year's stint in the Army, he won a cadetship to transfer as a trainee pilot to the RAAF base at Point Cook in Victoria. The next year he undertook a four-year service commission with the RAF in England.

It was in 1938 that he escaped death but not injury during a training flight crash, which put him in hospital for nine months with serious leg injuries. Only the start of the war and pilot shortages saved him from being invalided from the RAF and, by 1940, he was back in the air.

The subsequent achievements of Hughie Edwards are many and extraordinary, all epics of great courage and dauntless determination. Typical of them was the daylight raid he led targeting the German industrial city of Bremen in July 1941 when, in charge of 15 Blenheim bombers from two squadrons, he successfully completed the task in the face of a massive enemy offensive. Under his command, the bombers flew less than 16 metres above the sea and, upon reaching the coastline, hedge-hopped the remaining 80 kilometres to Bremen. Despite the planned element of surprise, the aircraft had been spotted at sea and the German defences forewarned of the impending attack. Thus the Blenheims had first to weave through a curtain of barrage balloons, then continue head-on into a huge wall of anti-aircraft gunfire and flak. As part of the low-level operation, the attacking planes also had to fly under high tension wires to drop bombs on the city's docklands. Four of the aircraft and their crews were lost.

After dropping his bombs, Edwards circled the city until all the Blenheims had unloaded theirs. He then led the remaining 11 planes back to England and was last to land. Later inspection showed predictable shell damage and not so predictable pieces of German telegraph wire hanging

*Edwards, always a man of action, even when visiting relatives in Melbourne during weekend breaks from training at Point Cook.*

from sections of the aircraft.

Soon after he was awarded the Victoria Cross, the citation noting that "Edwards displayed the highest possible standard of gallantry and determination."

His four DFCs and numerous other war decorations are some indication of one man's huge effort.

Edwards retired as an Air Commodore in 1963 and became chief executive of a Sydney-based mining company. In 1974 he was appointed Governor of WA, the year he was knighted, but retired 12 months later because of persistent poor health.

He died in Sydney on August 5, 1982

# Salvos' singing made for a rude awakening

Fremantle hotels
William Street, High Street
Map Ref: 43

**D**uring **March 1894,** the licensee of the Federal Hotel complained bitterly to the Fremantle Council that his house guests were "leaving in droves" because of the excessive noise coming from the adjacent Oddfellows Hall in William Street.

The butt of his complaint was the Salvation Army, presumably whose band and accompanying hymnal voices raised to God caused what the publican described as "an intolerable din" on weeknights and, more particularly one imagines, at 7 o'clock on Sunday mornings when the Salvos held their services. This unusual reversal of positions apparently was not resolved. As the Inquirer reported at the time, after some discussion the council decided it was "powerless to ameliorate any nuisance, if one existed," suggesting it was possibly a matter for the police.

Today, the Federal Hotel continues to trade in the colours of Rosie O'Grady's Irish Pub, but the basic exterior of the hotel, including the first floor verandah which overlooked Kings Square when the hotel was opened in 1887, has been restored as closely as possible to its original appearance.

Like other survivors in the central Fremantle streetscape, most of the hotels still serving the amber liquid have reinvented themselves variously since the halcyon days of the great gold rush which brought about their presence in the first place. Space does not permit more than a brief appraisal of how they have changed, and survived, while others have either been restored for other uses or disappeared altogether.

In the context of a Port city, most of the hotels served the needs of the waterfront, the lumpers generally crowding the front bars while the more well-to-do and white-collar employees, like customs and shipping agents, met and did business in the saloons. Women, be they so bold, might enter a ladies lounge, otherwise known as virgin parlours,

*Rosie O'Grady's Irish Pub*

*The Fremantle Hotel*

for a tipple. The hotels also served the business interests of the flourishing Fremantle community in the earlier days as well as providing accommodation for travellers arriving by ship or train.

The Fremantle Hotel, for example, built in 1898, originally had 100 guest rooms which, as an advertisement in The Morning Herald of that year described, "are furnished and arranged on the most modern principles and with perfect sanitary arrangements by which all refuse and waste water

*The Orient Hotel*

*The National Hotel*

clearing station, fitted out with tiered beds and an operating theatre. It was a matter of preparedness and, during those dark days, a high wall was built on the footpath outside the dining room area where the windows were boarded up. Regular exercises were held in preparation for anticipated air-raids. Fortunately, of course, there were no air-raids and no marine casualties. Meanwhile the bars stayed open and the beer continued to flow.

Further along High Street on the corner of Henry Street is the Orient Hotel which today has broad and popular appeal with karaoke and backpacker nights, pool competitions and live DJ. Established in 1901, this is another heritage-listed building described in earlier days as "a very grand hotel" and "the poshest in town," attracting many important patrons. Reflecting the new wealth and upper echelons of society of the times, its guests were expected to dress accordingly with collar and tie (indeed, hotel management kept spare jackets for those who might arrive without them). It was a well run hotel, with a fine dining room, a private entrance for guests and, like the Fremantle and the Federal, a separate sitting room for ladies.

Likewise, the National Hotel, on the corner of High and Market Streets was during its time recognised as one of the better residential hotels. Built in1895-6 on the site occupied previously by the National Bank of Australasia, over the years the National changed hands several times and became very much a pub for the working bloke and the port's lumpers. One publican, Irishman Jim Cranley, would celebrate St Patrick's Day by standing out on the pavement and buying every Irishman he met a beer, an annual ritual that ended, no doubt much to the disappointment of many men, when he returned to Ireland to die. His fortunes were in marked contrast to those of the first publican, William Conroy, who became the last person to be hanged in Perth Gaol for murdering a Fremantle councillor.

is carried direct to the sea." Notwithstanding subsequent changed attitudes to pollution, its continued elegant presence on the corner of Cliff and High Streets provides visual evidence of why the hotel was a favourite place, where master mariners stayed and those associated with shipping and port activity met for business and conviviality. This continued even during the days of World War II when the Navy occupied the guest rooms for officer accommodation and the dining room was transformed into Fremantle's premier casualty

# His music was a barbershop solo

Victoria Hall
179 High Street
Map Ref: 21

**T**he sound of a saxophone was not what clients expected to hear while they were having their hair cut at the barber's shop in William Street opposite Fremantle Town Hall. Nevertheless, the unmistakable notes from the sax drifting down from somewhere above would have prompted many a question about its source.

The barber, Bob Wrightson, no doubt explained that it was his son, Norman, practising his music in one of the rooms above, the apartment where they lived. The year was 1934 and the young lad was barely 11 years old. Remarkably, in just another four years he would have formed his own five-piece band, earning 8/6d (85cents) a night playing music at local dances.

The story of Norm Wrightson and his elder brother Robert is part of Fremantle folklore. These two highly talented young men went on to make big names for themselves in the entertainment world - Norm, as a virtuoso of the saxophone and clarinet, and Robert as a world-class exhibition ballroom dancer and teacher.

While they were both trained as hairdressers, Robert's love of dancing took him away from the family business when he and his wife Shelda opened their first professional dance studio in 1945. Norm, however, continued to work as a hairdresser and maintain the family business right through until retirement at the age of 75.

There was a common power-base to this twin talent which served both brothers admirably throughout their musical years

- and remains a public icon to this day. It is Victoria Hall in High Street, one of the great surviving landmarks of early Fremantle, and another splendid example of a John Talbot Hobbs design.

It was here that Robert and Shelda Wrightson established the Wrightson Dance Studio, first leasing then later buying the building. It was here one Saturday night in 1949 that Norm Wrightson's Orchestra began a fashion in full swing before a packed hall. It was altogether a family affair, the brothers' father acting as doorman and their mother running the ticket office. From that first night, Saturday dancing became a regular and enormously popular feature of the Fremantle scene.

Thus began a long era through the 1950s and beyond when Victoria Hall was the major attraction for thousands of locals, as well as visiting sailors, not to mention bodgies and widgies from Perth, who danced - and not infrequently brawled - the night away to the sound of Norm Wrightson's five piece band.

It was a busy time for both Wrightsons. Robert and Shelda were by now heavily involved in competition as well as teaching and opening up other studios, which took them to other Australian States and overseas. On top of winning many titles, including State and Australasian professional ballroom championships, in 1952 they were the first

Australians to win the British open and the world exhibition championship at Blackpool, England.

Norm Wrightson's Orchestra was in great demand, playing almost nightly at various locations and occasions, weddings included. When brother Robert and partners launched a new ballroom in Perth - Canterbury Court in Beaufort Street - another new Saturday night era began, and lasted for many years. As a saxophonist-clarinet player, Norm was also called on to help provide big band backing for visiting artists like Nat King Cole and Pat Boone, among others. It was a period when five hours of sleep a night seemed a luxury, wedged between packing up the band after midnight and opening up the barber's shop at daybreak.

*Norm Wrightson, left, with musician Harry Bluck.*

Meanwhile, unlike the music and the virtual demise of the Saturday night dance, Victoria Hall survived, despite several attempts to have it demolished as it fell into disrepair. Both before and after those mid-years of its existence, the building has been used in many different ways - for theatre productions, as a meeting place for the Communist Party, as a scout hall, a venue for boxing and even a thrift shop. Built as a parish hall by St John's Church in 1896 at the height of the goldrush, it was originally named St John's Hall, but, rather like South Quay and its subsequent name change, was renamed the following year to commemorate Queen Victoria's Silver Jubilee.

After much wrangling about its future and considerable support from local people and organisations, the City of Fremantle bought the building in 2001 from Robert Wrightson (who in turn had bought it from St John's Parish in 1971) and implemented a restoration programme. Now listed with the National Trust and the national and State heritage registers, Victoria Hall will once again be assured of its future for the benefit of the community at large.

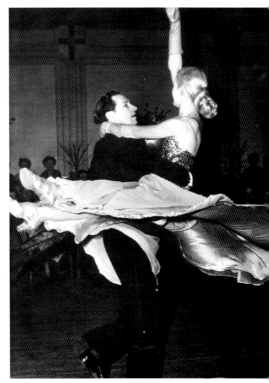

*Robert Wrightson and his wife Shelda... they reached the peak of international success.*

# The prison superintendent who fell from grace

Fremantle Prison
The Terrace
Map Ref: 22

**F**remantle Prison had a rocky start. Not only did the Prison itself have to be hacked out of a limestone hill - its first Superintendent, Thomas Hill Dixon, was dismissed in disgrace for embezzlement.

The Swan River Colony was established in 1829 as a free settlement. But after 20 years the future of the colony was threatened by a big population decline and labour shortage. The colonists sought a radical solution. In 1849 the British Government was asked to create a 'regular penal settlement' with a convict establishment to maintain and supervise the convicts. The convict labour force would be used for public works - building roads, bridges and public buildings - while a ticket-of-leave scheme would provide the colony with reformed men, trained to become permanent colonists.

The first convicts arrived off Fremantle on June 1, 1850 on *Scindian*, a fast Indiaman. Aboard were 75 convicts, 50 pensioner guards with their wives and families, some passengers with their families and servants and a small party of officials, warders, sappers and miners under Comptroller General, Captain Edmund Henderson. Also on board was Thomas Dixon and his family. Dixon, a complex person who faced perennial financial and marital problems, was born in 1816 on the Isle of Man.

Medicine was his first career choice but he never completed his training. He became a police constable in London in 1842 before deciding to start a new life in the Australian colonies. He joined the Convict Service and within three years had been appointed Superintendent of convicts in remote Western Australia.

*Scindian's* journey was too fast. It overtook vessels that were expected to warn the colony of the convicts' arrival and with the Round House too small, no arrangements had been made to accommodate them. Henderson hired a warehouse from local merchant and Harbour Master Daniel Scott and adapted it to hold the convicts. This temporary accommodation, on the site now occupied by the Esplanade Hotel, was used for five years.

After organising a temporary prison Henderson had to select a permanent site. His first choice was where Perth's iconic Kings Park is now.

But the Governor and his advisers frowned on having a convict institution in the midst of the capital city. A more appropriate site was selected in 1851 in Fremantle - a safer 20km from Perth and Government House. The prison's four-storey main cell block - the biggest convict-built structure in WA - was constructed under instruction from the Royal Engineers, between 1852 and 1859 though convicts moved into the southern half in June 1855.

By the standards of the time, Dixon was an enlightened administrator. He strongly disapproved of flogging and created a regime that was more humane than those in English prisons of the time. His attitudes were helped by the reason for convicts being in the colony - as labourers and ultimately, hopefully permanent settlers. Punishment through suffering was never an objective and Dixon worked to maintain this distinction. By the end of 1857, of the 1233 convicts who had been sent to the colony, 20 per cent had been given tickets-of-leave to join the labour market. Due mainly to Dixon's policies the Convict Establishment was training 'tolerable' blacksmiths, carpenters, rough-masons, tailors and shoemakers.

But while his role as an administrator was praised and respected, his personal life was full of problems. The year after arriving on *Scindian* the woman who accompanied him as his 'wife' was banished to Toodyay "for the benefit of the service." In April 1859 Dixon - who was described as a hard-working and trusted officer and Henderson's right-hand man - was suspended from his position after admitting embezzling public and private funds. He was tried and imprisoned after being found to be a debtor to the Crown but released in July after legal argument that the case against him was flawed.

Dixon then made his way to Labuan Island off Borneo where he was appointed chief constable but was asked to resign after the Colonial Office heard about his problems in WA. He then headed to China where he became a mercenary and was involved in the attack on Shanghai in 1862. By 1865 he was back in England. With his two daughters married and living in WA, Dixon, his health declining, decided to join them, returning to WA in 1876. He died in 1880 on the property of his eldest daughter Mary and her husband Stephen Monger - recognition of his achievements eroded by his inability to live within his means.

Fremantle Prison
The Terrace
Map Ref: 22

*John Boyle O'Reilly - the first convict to escape from Swan River Colony who went on to become a legend in the USA.*

**A** **dramatic nautical standoff in the Indian Ocean** off the coast of Western Australia in 1876 almost brought the Swan River Colony, then a mere 47 years old, to war with the United States of America. The tense confrontation between the American whaler, *Catalpa*, and the English-built steamer, *Georgette*, was defused by American bluff and a backdown by cautious WA officials. As a result *Catalpa* sailed back to America with six Irish convicts who had made the most daring escape in WA history.

The former Superintendent of Fremantle Prison, Henry Maxwell Lefroy, wrote to his brother in England: *"We have just had a very exciting event in the escape from the colony of six of the principal Fenian military prisoners. They were carried off by an American vessel,* Catalpa, *ostensibly a whaler, but really chartered and fitted out by the Fenian headquarters for this special project. The British Government detectives in America had discovered this project and communicated it to the Foreign Office (in London), which again warned our Governor of it. The latter contented himself with warning the (prison) Controller who again did nothing whatever to meet and defeat the plot. I guess that both he and the Governor will get a very unpleasant wigging (reprimand) from the Colonial Office later on."*

The Fenian movement, or Irish Republican Brotherhood, was a secret society that flourished during the 1860s. Its activities included a failed armed rebellion against British rule in Ireland. In 1865 hundreds of men suspected of being involved were arrested in Ireland. The following year, John Boyle O'Reilly, a trained journalist but then an NCO in the 10th Hussars, was sentenced to death at a court martial for helping fellow soldiers join the Fenians. His sentence was commuted to 20 years' penal servitude and he was transported to WA on *Hougoumont* with 280 other convicts, 62 of them Fenians, arriving in January 1868.

O'Reilly, sent to work near Bunbury, engineered his escape in 1869 on an American whaler. He eventually made his way to Boston where he became a respected citizen and editor of The Pilot, the biggest Catholic newspaper in the world. However, he did not forget his fellow Fenians languishing in Fremantle Prison and gathered support for a rescue attempt. With funds raised by the Irish secret society Clan na Gael in America and eastern Australia, a cargo ship, *Catalpa*, was purchased and refitted as a whaler under the command of George Anthony.

*The New Bedford whaler Catalpa and its skipper, Captain George Anthony*

On March 29 1876 *Catalpa* berthed at Bunbury. In the meantime Americans John Breslin and Thomas Desmond, posing as wealthy businessmen, had been in Fremantle setting up the escape. *Catalpa* moved up the coast offshore between Rottnest and Garden Islands. On Easter Monday, April 17, contact was made with the six Fenian prisoners in work parties outside the Prison. They rendezvoused with two horse-drawn buggies outside the Prison, rushed to the waterfront at Rockingham and transferred to an open whaleboat.

A timber company worker witnessed the transfer and his suspicions aroused, rode to Fremantle to alert the authorities. A fast police cutter sent to Rockingham arrived only in time to see the whaleboat heading to the horizon. The cutter returned to Fremantle and *Georgette* was commissioned to help. In the meantime the Fenians, unable in the gathering darkness to link up with *Catalpa*, were forced to spend an uncomfortable unscheduled night at sea. The following day the cutter and *Georgette*, under the command of the Superintendent of Water Police, J.F. Stone, resumed the search. *Georgette* finally made contact with *Catalpa* and Stone asked to be allowed on board to check for escapees. His request was denied and *Georgette*, running low on coal, was forced to return to Fremantle.

By 2pm the refuelled *Georgette* - now armed with a 12-pound howitzer canon on its front deck - spotted the whaleboat approaching *Catalpa* and gave chase. But the escapees eluded it and were hauled aboard *Catalpa* which immediately set sail for open waters. It was not until 8am on April 19 that *Georgette* overtook *Catalpa*, calling on it to stop. Shots were fired across its stern and bow. *Catalpa* hove-to but the wily Anthony claimed they were in international waters under the American flag. He challenged Stone to create a diplomatic incident - and possibly provoke a war with Britain - if he dared. Uncertain, Stone reluctantly let *Catalpa* - and the Fenians - sail away. They arrived in New York to a tumultuous reception in August 1876.

*Catalpa* ended its days as a coal barge in British Honduras. *Georgette* was not so lucky. Bound for Adelaide on her final voyage she was wrecked in December 1876 off the mouth of the Margaret River. Sixteen-year-old Grace Bussell and Aboriginal stockman Sam Isaacs were awarded bravery medals for rescuing survivors.

O'Reilly, the first convict to escape from the Swan River Colony, was also its first novelist (Moondyne Joe) and US President John F. Kennedy's favourite poet. He never left Boston. He died in 1890 and his funeral was reputed to have been the biggest in US history until that for Kennedy - another Bostonian - in 1963.

The *Catalpa* escape had taken four years to organise, covered 48,000km and cost $US25,000. And *Hougoumont* was the last ship to bring convicts to the Swan River Colony - and Australia.

# The prisoner who phoned his mother for a recipe

Fremantle Prison
The Terrace
Map Ref: 22

**F**remantle Prison was no holiday camp. Built initially to house convicts from Britain, then home to Western Australia's worst offenders, it was hot in summer - despite its elevated position - cold in winter and often overcrowded. From 1888 it was the only place of legal execution in the State. One Prison chief said that being in Fremantle Prison was always a brutalising experience.

Unrest among prisoners - often via protests, demonstrations and riots - was not uncommon and escaping was never far from their minds. Many tried and some succeeded but usually not for long.

The escape described as the most remarkable in the history of the WA Prison system, occurred in relatively recent times. The following year Royal Commissioner Judge Robert Jones said it was one of the most remarkable stories ever to emerge from any prison in the world and attached phrases such as "rather eccentric genius" and "devious ingenuity" to its mastermind, Owen Hooper.

The escape took 12 months to plan and involved two other prisoners, William Cabalt and Stanley Stone, who said that they feared for their lives if they stayed in prison any longer. Hooper was an excellent electronics technician. Cabalt was his assistant and Stone shared a cell with Cabalt. Hooper and Cabalt were in charge of the Prison radio broadcast cell which relayed music to the cells. They also had an adjoining cell equipped as a workshop in which they could carry out electronic repair work for Prison staff and charitable organisations.

In 1971 Hooper tapped into the hospital's telephone system, then constructed a listening and dialing mechanism from spares in the electronics workshop. When hospital staff left for the day Hooper and Cabalt used the device to dial out. They telephoned radio stations and made music requests and Hooper rang old school friends and even his mother to ask for her scrambled eggs recipe.

Hooper next obtained details about a French Government weather balloon tracking project. After receiving permission from the Prison authorities to join the project he constructed a receiving set that could monitor signals from the balloons. Hooper claimed that interference from the radio cell made monitoring difficult and convinced the authorities to let him have another cell on the top floor of New

*LEFT: The doors are open now, but once the cells of the refractory block (commonly known as solitary confinement) accommodated some of the State's toughest criminals.*

Photo courtesy West Australian Newspapers

*The 1988 riots, when fires and violence caused more than $1 million damage.*

Division. The telephone line was then transferred to the new cell.

Joined by Stone they next put a hole in the ceiling of the cell. Early on a dark and rainy July morning in 1972 they climbed through the ceiling to the end of New Division and broke a hole in the asbestos roof. Now in the open, they were in view of two armed guards, particularly one at the No. 2 gun post, less than 50 metres away. Using a field telephone he had earlier put together Hooper rang the guard at the No. 2 post and said: *"Gate officer here. Some suspicious activity has been observed down near the back of the Carpenter's Shop. Keep an eye on it for the next few minutes."*

With the officer distracted the trio retrieved the ladder they had made from plaited telephone cable, crossed to the wall and slipped down the opposite side into Knutsford Street to a waiting getaway car organised earlier via their illegal telephone. They were recaptured in October 1972.

Then there was the so-called Butter Incident in the 1970s when a prisoner used angel wire - diamond-encrusted wire that can be hidden in a shoelace - to cut through the end bar of his top floor cell window. He lubricated the next bar along with butter and managed to squeeze through the gap. He then ran along the roof of New Division, jumped across the narrow space between the end of the division and the platform of an unmanned guard post, slipped over the wall and into Holdsworth Street below. Later that night, arrested in Perth for vagrancy, he said he was an escapee from Fremantle Prison. However, the police were not sure. They rang the main gate at the Prison and asked if anyone was missing. Prison officers looked in his cell and said the prisoner was still in his bed. At 2.30am the next

day the police, still suspicious, went to the Prison and asked that the cell be checked again. This time the cell was opened and a dummy found in the bed. Four prison officers were later charged with dereliction of duty.

Another more notorious escapee, the so-called Postcard Bandit, Brenden Abbott, is reputed to have returned to the Prison in 1992 while on the run and signed the visitors' book - Name: *B. Abbett(sic)*. Address: *Nowhere you'd find!* Remarks: *"Great to come back and not have to escape."* Handwriting tests were conducted but nothing was conclusive. And then there was the prisoner, very close to release, who was involved in repair work on top of a wall. Unnoticed, he slipped and fell into Holdsworth Street, then walked around to the front gate and asked to be readmitted. Initially he was not believed because no alarm had been raised.

The Prison has also had its share of protests - inside and out. During a riot in the overcrowded Prison in 1968, shots were fired when about 500 prisoners refused to return to their cells after an exercise period. The worst - and last - protest before the Prison was closed in 1991 was the violent riot of 1988 which caused extensive damage. In a spell of very hot weather in January that year inmates stormed the main cell block, savagely attacked prison officers and lit fires in cells. Five officers were taken hostage. The incident lasted through the night and into the next day and the damage bill topped $1 million.

# Gangster Ryan kept the prison clock ticking

Fremantle Prison gates and clock
The Terrace
Map Ref: 22

**F**or much of its history the clock over the main gates at Fremantle Prison was notoriously unreliable.

The clock, brought from England, was installed in the tower over the gatehouse in 1856. However, for about 60 years, until the mid-1930s, it had not worked properly, if at all. The man who fixed it was the criminal with "brains in his fingertips," Ernest 'Shiner' Ryan, an eastern States gangster who later became part of Fremantle folklore.

Ryan not only mastered the clock but on release left written instructions on how to keep it working. These were found in the 1960s by an apprentice plumber whose access to repair a leaking roof was via the clocktower.

The first Comptroller-General of Prisons in Western Australia, Captain Edmund Henderson had been given a grant of about 36 acres (14.5ha) of land in a prime position to establish the Prison. Pleased with the location, Henderson wrote: "the site proposed is in every way well suited for the purpose; it is a healthy and elevated spot - removed from the business part of the town and within convenient distance of the harbour."

*One of Ryan's porridge boats, mounted on a 'sea' of broken bottle pieces.*

Work on the prison began in 1852 under the instruction of the Royal Engineers and was completed in 1859. By the time the transportation of convicts from Britain ended in 1868 almost 10,000 convicts had been sent to WA. In 1886, with less than 50 convicts still imprisoned, the British Government passed control of the Prison to the colonial government and Fremantle Prison became the Swan River Colony's primary place of incarceration. The Perth Gaol, built by convicts in the 1850s, was closed and all its inmates, including women, transferred to Fremantle.

Ryan found his way into the Prison in late 1932 but had a long history of crime behind him by the time he got to WA. Born in South Australia in 1887 his first recorded conviction was in Adelaide in 1902 for larceny. He was whipped and ordered to be detained in a reformatory until the age of 18. He later racked up a string of convictions for relatively minor crimes in three States before graduating to the big-time. In Sydney in 1914 Ryan was the brains behind the Everleigh Railway Workshops robbery - the first payroll robbery in Australia and the first where a motor vehicle was used in the getaway. More than 3,300 pounds ($6,600) were stolen and Ryan received a 10-year sentence.

By the time he got to WA he had downsized to picking shop locks (which he could do with his back to the lock so he could keep watch) and stealing stock. Fremantle Prison brought out his creative side. Apart from being the only person who knew how to keep the clock running on time, he built his famous porridge boats (one of which is on display at the Prison), painted The Reclamation, depicting Christ holding a black sheep with the prison gates in the background, and is alleged to have made counterfeit 2-shilling (20c) pieces in the metal workshop which were briefly passed as currency in Fremantle.

In appreciation of the treatment he had received in the Fremantle Hospital in wartime 1941, Ryan got the idea of making V for Victory badges from a discarded bath heater and selling them to help the hospital's X-ray appeal. In a letter to the assistant secretary of the Hospital in 1941, Ryan wrote: *"Those Vs represent the disintegration of a gas bath heater...... The (Prison) Superintendent (Mr A. Dickson) had a brand new nickel-plated bath water heater recently installed for his house and as I was running out of material for the making of the Vs I suggested to him that he could take me out to his house to have a peep at his nice new heater. To this suggestion Mr Dickson said: 'You're not going to get your hands onto my bath heater.' Sir, what does the Superintendent's reply imply?"*

For his porridge boats, Ryan carved sailing boat replicas from wood, plastered them with porridge, blew finely-powdered glass over them and mounted them on a 'sea' of blue castor-oil bottle pieces. Out of gaol, Ryan was also involved in the invention and marketing of war-time kerosene candles and used his skills to mend watches, clocks, bicycles and toys.

In 1950 Ryan married infamous Sydney underworld figure Kate Leigh, who had also been involved by association in the Everleigh robbery, at St John's Church, Fremantle. He left for Sydney but returned without his bride soon after. He quietly lived his remaining years in Fremantle. Ryan died in 1957, a liked and respected member of the Fremantle community. His funeral was attended by the mayors of Fremantle and East Fremantle. Ryan, who had spent most of his 71 years in gaol (by the time he was 54 his sentences tallied 43 years), had become a legendary criminal, revered among his peers as a pioneer of hold-up techniques and as the grandmaster of lock pickers.

When Fremantle Prison closed in 1991 Ryan was just one of an estimated 250,000 convicts and other prisoners who had passed through its gates since 1855.

# These tunnels helped solve a water problem

Fremantle Prison
The Terrace
Map Ref: 22

**O**ne of the little-known but impressive and once important features of Fremantle Prison are the reservoirs and tunnels hacked out of the limestone underneath by prisoners more than 100 years ago.

In a continent as dry as Australia water has always been a scarce and valuable commodity. The establishment of the European settlement at Fremantle soon exposed water problems. In 1829, soon after the founding of the Swan River Colony, Royal Navy Lieutenant Breton described Fremantle as ".....a mere encampment, every person being in a tent or temporary hut....water was easily procured by digging holes a few feet in depth but it was not particularly good." In 1830 Mary Ann Friend wrote: "We are always thirsty, always drinking and never satisfied." Fremantle depended on wells and springs for many years.

However, the growing population and the demand from shipping, government establishments and businesses meant that other sources had to be found.

The first well had been sunk at Fremantle Prison in 1852. More were sunk to provide a plentiful and reliable supply. Pumps were imported from England and hand-operated by prisoners sentenced to hard labour. Soon there was wider demand for the Prison water. A jetty had been built at Fremantle in 1867 and seven years later Prison wells were providing water for ships and some other places in the town including the Railway Station. The water was pumped manually by prisoners to storage areas where it then gravitated to the town. In one year prisoners pumped 12 million gallons. The West Australian Times noted that "....in the winter the rain diverted from the roof of the Prison will lessen the labour of pumping." Two substantial barrel-vaulted brick reservoirs were built in the Prison compound, one in 1876 and another in the early 1890s.

By 1880 the people of Fremantle wanted Prison water to be provided to the whole town. A new well was sunk in the Prison yard. From the bottom of this, prisoners built tunnels, shafts and drives connected to the three wells on the eastern side of the site. The water was pumped to the reservoirs and then into the town. Steam engines were put into operation, day and night. This took the pumping chore off the prisoners who then had to chop the wood to keep the engines going. By 1888 the townspeople had the reliable source they had sought, making Fremantle the first reticulated district in the Colony.

The amazing tunnel network is still in good condition and adventurous tourists will soon be able to explore them in specially constructed boats. Visitor access to the tunnels is via a series of ladders and landings. About 20m below the surface the water in the 1.5m x 2m tunnels is clear enough for people to see the silty bottom littered with pieces of timber and metal used in the construction. The tunnels were completed in 1898 and used until 1910 when a dam was built to supply scheme water to the metropolitan area. The water under the Prison increasingly became brackish and contaminated with oil in 1989. The oil spill was cleaned up by 1996. The reservoir and the pumping station remain within the Prison walls but are no longer used.

One of the first things constructed on the original 14.5ha of land set aside for the Convict Establishment site was a ramp (later Fairbairn Street) which was fitted with metal rail tracks used to haul materials up the hill to the building site. North of the ramp on ground which now takes in the Parry Street carpark, a vegetable garden was established. An ingenious watering system was developed. Prison authorities noted: "The privies (in the Prison) will be flushed twice a day by the water from the baths, washing sheds and cells and the manure in a highly-

diluted state applied to the garden ground." However, a filtering system intended to purify the waste was not particularly effective and the drains were a constant source of smells, mosquitoes and suspected illness for some decades until the prison was connected to the town sewage system in 1922.

South of the ramp the Enrolled Pensioner Guards used the area between the gardens and their barracks as a parade and drill ground. In 1894 this land was granted to the Fremantle Council as a public recreation ground and named Fremantle Oval. In the 19th century the main cell block was the longest and tallest prison building in the southern hemisphere. The Prison site now covers about 6ha and receives more than 130,000 visitors each year.

*Top: Tree roots exposed 17 metres below street level appear like strange stalactites in one of the dry sections of the tunnel network.*

*Centre: Boating beneath the prison... the new tunnel experience.*

*Bottom: The reservoir which supplied Fremantle with water and (inset) one of the hand-operated valves connecting the system.*

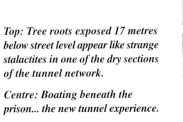

## Fremantle Oval
## Parry Street
## Map Ref: 23

**B**eing sent to school in Adelaide was a defining move for Fremantle boys Bill Bateman and Harry Herbert - and for sport in Western Australia.

They came back from Prince Alfred College enthusiastic about a new form of football which was spreading from Victoria and were determined to introduce it to WA. Until the 1880s, football was played under rugby rules or a variation of them by Englishmen or colonists with strong links, often through education and family, to England and to rugby.

But the return from Adelaide of Bateman and Herbert - the sons of Fremantle merchants and shipowners with a stronger attachment to their new country than the 'motherland' - changed that. In 1883 they called a meeting in Fremantle to form a port club playing the rules developed in Victoria in the late 1850s. However, it was not until the club's annual general meeting, at the Cleopatra Hotel in 1885, that the move gained momentum. Bateman was elected captain of the team which became the Fremantle Football Club and a majority decided in favour of playing the Australian game. Soon after other clubs followed and the WA Football Association was established.

Bateman, now regarded as the 'Father of WA Football', was a grandson of John Bateman who had arrived in Fremantle in 1830. A champion sportsman and pioneer of the Bull Creek/Melville area, he represented WA in both football and cricket and was an inaugural inductee into the WA Football Hall of Fame.

The new game was played on an area which began as a parade ground for convict guards and was then known as Barrack Green or Barrack Field. The site had been gazetted in 1851 as part of the crown grant allocated for the development of the Convict Establishment in Fremantle. In 1853 a barrack to house 32 Enrolled Pensioner Guards and their families was built and part of the area next to the barrack used as a parade drill ground. The guards came to the colony after the British Government was asked to strengthen what was regarded as a weak military presence in the colony. It replied that because of the disturbed state of politics in Europe it was not prepared to increase the number of troops. However, it suggested that WA take advantage of the availability of military pensioners and use them as an auxiliary force to the regulars.

A voluntary militia corp, the Fremantle Volunteer Rifles, formed in 1862, also used the Green for muster and drill duty and the volunteers and their band provided some of the early entertainment for Fremantle residents. The Green was also used for recreational football (rugby) before the advent of the Australian Rules competition in 1885.

*A cycling event at Fremantle Oval in 1910.*
*The track was laid in 1898.*

The Pensioner Guard force was disbanded in the 1880s and the Green became largely unused open space, apart from football matches and general recreational use. In 1893 Fremantle sporting clubs and the council sought State Government approval to have the Green set aside as a public recreation ground. This was done in 1894 and the following year an agreement was signed between the council and the Fremantle and Imperial Football Clubs setting out conditions for the use of the grounds. The first game was played on the newly-established oval in May, 1895.

The council improved the ground to cater for football, cricket and cycling which was an immensely popular sport in Fremantle. It was not until 1964 that the track around the oval - a major cycling competition venue - was removed. In the late 1890s the oval hosted a cricket match between an Australian eleven and an English team passing through Fremantle to play a Test series in the Eastern States.

The oval was also used regularly for community activities and public celebrations. Its central position and size also made it an excellent venue for civic ceremonies and celebrations to mark significant events at the State, national or international level. In February, 1900 thousands attended a special rally to mark the departure of Australian military contingents to the Boer War. A year later another huge crowd celebrated the inauguration of the Commonwealth of Australia.

In 1919 the oval was chosen as the site to discharge soldiers returning from World War I. It had been intended to restrict civilians from the oval but it was reported that "by 3.30 (pm) there were more civilians than soldiers within the enclosure and the marquees were literally bursting with impatient men eager to be fitted up and away."

In 1927 the oval was used to welcome the Duke (later King George VI) and Duchess of York to WA. Twenty seven years later it served the same purpose for their daughter, Queen Elizabeth II and her husband, the Duke of Edinburgh.

After World War II interest in all sports increased but football matches drew particularly big crowds. Football was seen as a force which contributed to Fremantle's sense of community identity and the development of the oval was a central part of port life. The Fremantle teams were also among the most successful in the WA football competition. The oval's football connection was further strengthened in 1994 when it became the host ground for the Fremantle Dockers - the second WA club to be admitted to the Australian Football League.

The construction of the Parry Street extension in 1986 - part of preparations for the America's Cup defence in 1987 - had a major impact on the oval site and the Victoria Pavilion which now backs onto the street. The pavilion, named in honour of Queen Victoria, was built in 1897 - the 60th year of her reign - and was described at the time as a handsome structure with seating for 1200 people. It was heritage-listed in 1993.

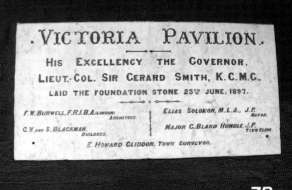

. VICTORIA PAVILION .

HIS EXCELLENCY THE GOVERNOR,
LIEUT.-COL. SIR GERARD SMITH, K.C.M.C.,
LAID THE FOUNDATION STONE 25TH JUNE, 1897.

F. W. BURWELL, F.R.I.B.A.(LONDON)     ELIAS SOLOMON, M.L.A., J.P.
ARCHITECT.     MAYOR

C.W. AND S. BLACKMAN,     MAJOR C. BLAND HUMBLE, J.P.
BUILDERS.     TOWN CLERK.

E. HOWARD CLIDDON, TOWN SURVEYOR.

# Edmund Henderson, from Fremantle Prison to Scotland Yard

The Knowle, Fremantle Hospital
Corner of South Terrace and Alma Street
Map Ref: 24

**A**lmost hidden in the centre of the sprawling grounds of Fremantle Hospital is The Knowle, a large and striking building of round arches and latticed verandahs which had its beginnings in the early convict days of Western Australia. The elegant two-storey home was designed by the State's first Comptroller General of Convicts, Edmund Henderson, to house his wife and young son. The building

*The Knowle - as it used to be when it became Fremantle Hospital.*

was completed in 1852, two years after the Henderons arrived in Fremantle in the sailing ship *Scindian*, along with 75 convicts and warders and their families - the first such shipment from England to WA.

The Knowle was centrally located close to convict establishments - the first temporary quarters near Essex Street followed, in 1859, by the Imperial Convict Establishment (later Fremantle Prison). It wasn't until almost another 40 years that The Knowle's role changed dramatically - from a house to a hospital - which it has remained ever since a matron and a handful of nursing staff moved there in 1897. The hospital then comprised 52 beds, accommodating patients transferred from the Point Street Pensioner Hospital nearby.

*Edmund Henderson*

For Edmund Henderson, his association with Fremantle was a major part of an extraordinary career. The son of an English Vice-Admiral, Edmund Yeamans Walcott Henderson received a commission in the Royal Engineers in 1838 and, the following year, was sent to Canada to assist with boundary surveys of territory ceded by the United States. He was still only 18 years of age, but his stint in North America gave him considerable early experience and a reputation as a surveyor and draughtsman. After completion of one of his last assignments - to determine the practicality of building a railway between Halifax and Quebec - he returned to England in 1848. Two years later he was on the move again, this time to Western Australia with his Canadian-born wife Mary. He was still aged only 29.

He served two terms in Australia - from 1850-1856 and from 1858-1863. During his first stint he designed and oversaw the construction of the Fremantle Prison and the warders cottages, as well as the Lunatic Asylum and, of course, The Knowle. More important, as the person with overall responsibility for the convicts he seemed to have adopted a more humane approach to their treatment and welfare than would some of his successors. An entry in a rules and regulations book he compiled for prison officers gives some insight into that, one excerpt reading: *It is the duty of all officers to treat the prisoners with kindness and humanity, and to listen patiently to and report their complaints or grievances: being firm at the same time in maintaining discipline and order, and enforcing complete observance of the Rules and Regulations of the Establishment.*

It was during his first term in Western Australia that his wife Mary, whom he'd wed in Nova Scotia in 1848, suddenly became ill and died. She was buried in the Skinner Street cemetery and, although her headstone cannot be found, her remains were probably removed and reburied in the Fremantle Cemetery in Carrington Street.

Henderson remarried a year after returning to England and his second wife, Maria Hindle, returned with him to resume residence at The Knowle for the next five years. While his position was still Comptroller General of Convicts, his responsibilities as a senior officer in the Royal Engineers had spread beyond to the early establishment of public works in WA. He was promoted to the rank of Lieut. Colonel by the time he left Fremantle .

If Henderson left his mark on Fremantle, so did he on his country of birth. On return to England in 1863, he was appointed Surveyor-General of Prisons and later became Chief Commissioner of the London Metropolitan Police (the Met). Equally significantly, perhaps, he helped establish the Criminal Investigation Department (CID), today better known as Scotland Yard. For his many outstanding efforts, Henderson was knighted in 1878.

He died in London in 1896. And while his name means little to most people today beyond the street and district named after him, the man behind The Knowle provided Fremantle with a functional piece of heritage which remains a visible reminder of a remarkable career.

# A perfect season at the seaside

South Beach
Ocean Drive, South Fremantle
Map Ref: 41

The quiet stretch of green parkland and ocean beach just south of Fremantle holds countless stories and memories of the time when this was the most popular resort in Western Australia.

South Beach was already called the 'Brighton of the West' by 1902, when thousands thronged the beach for the official annual opening of the season. For more than five decades it remained the magnet for multitudes of families from Perth and beyond

*The Hydrodome in the 1920s.*

who flocked there by train during the summer to enjoy the seaside experience and its multiple offerings.

During weekends and holiday times, they would arrive in droves with their picnic baskets and bathers for a day's outing. There was much to do and see. A shark-proof net guaranteed safe swimming and the adjacent Hydrodome provided all sorts of facilities and entertainment for a perfect day out. The large two-storey building - formerly a part of Fremantle Base Hospital relocated to the beach in 1923 - had a kiosk, tea rooms, change rooms as well as a ballroom and an area for roller-skating. If you forgot your bathers you could hire them at the Hydrodome. If you didn't like the water, you could just walk the jetty and take in the sights. At the end of the jetty were diving boards and a slippery dip for the more active ocean-goers. Back on the foreshore, a sideshow alley added to the carnival atmosphere. Locals performed circus tricks and there were merry-go-rounds and slot machines. So much to do and see.

A Fremantle Council tourist guide of 1911 is almost euphoric in its description of: 'Bright, Breezy, Bracing South Beach,' going on to extol its virtues ". . . from breakfast to bedtime there is movement and music, fun and frolic, for this South Beach is a wonderful playground for children; the very sea seems to enjoy it, and sparkles with excitement . . . the beach is safe, and the delights of wading and shell gathering, as well as the many other exclusive seaside pleasures, occupy the mind . . . the medicinal breezes strengthening the body."

In such a wholesome environment it is easy to imagine the council's consternation some 28 years earlier when, in those days of neck-to-knees beachwear, skinny-dipping had already found a place at the beach. At a monthly meeting on December 5, 1893, item 16 of correspondence noted that "Councillor Marshall drew attention to the practice of bathing along the South Beach without any bathing costume whatever as late as 7 and 8 o'clock in the morning. It was decided that the police be communicated with on the matter."

*Cover of Fremantle Council's 1911 tourist booklet.*

While South Beach was so good for the human condition, it also identified strongly with equine excellence, for it was on this stretch of beach that WA's first official horse race was held, in October 1833, an event that has been re-enacted regularly. During the 1920s and the 1930s, more than 30 trainers from nearby stables used the beach daily to train their horses. This would attract much curiosity, particularly on Saturday mornings when several hundred onlookers would gather to watch the horses being taken from South Beach by train to the races. The local stables produced some of the top riders and horses of the time who went on to win many of Australia's premier races. Not surprisingly, South Beach may justifiably be considered the birthplace of horse racing in WA.

The interruption of World War II and the many post-war changes in community lifestyle and needs began the decline of South Beach as a major resort. This was further impacted by the weathering nature of time and

*Crowds watch a sailing regatta at South Beach, 1920.*

tide which caused serious beach erosion and damage to facilities, including the destruction of the jetty. In 1956, a big storm cut several metres into the beach, sweeping away many of the big foreshore pine trees, destroying shelter sheds and damaging the sea wall. In 1964, the remaining lower level of the Hydrodome was taken away, the top storey already having been dissembled earlier as a result of white ant damage. Its removal was almost the last visible link with the South Beach many thousands of people once knew, and enjoyed so much in its halcyon days.

Despite these earlier setbacks, today the beach is still a popular place for families, well served by a busy kiosk, ample parking and Fremantle's free bus service. The council has done much to restore the parklands as well as beach and swimming facilities. Beyond the southern groyne is an extensive walkway where people can take their pets to chase along the incoming tide. And, whatever the future may hold, South Beach will remain a people's place - and one of the best spots along the coast for watching the sun sink below the Indian Ocean on a summer's night.

# Jon conquered - and discovered - ocean mountains

WA Maritime Museum
Victoria Quay
Map Ref: 25

**O**f the many spectacular displays at Fremantle's Maritime Museum, there is one that never fails to grab everyone's attention and spark great wonderment.

The yacht is pitched precariously at 35 degrees, with bow pointed down at the floor and the rope of the sea-brake snaking out from the stern metres above to the high ceiling. Its sole occupant clings desperately to the mast. This is *Parry Endeavour*, authentic in every detail except for the life-size model of Jon Sanders.

The courage and high drama of Sanders' single handed, non-stop voyage three times around the globe is well documented and the museum display depicts one of the most extraordinary moments of the 658-day epic - when the 14-metre sloop ran into horrendous gale force winds in the Southern Ocean and was frequently swept crashing down 30-metre waves like an oversize surfboard. For the former sheep shearer, whose love of sailing began with paddling his canoe as an eight-year old in the Swan River and hero worship of Captain James Cook, this was certainly a defining moment.

For the average landlubber, the prospect of taking on a hermit existence would be no small challenge. But doing it at sea added new dimensions of scale and preparation. This, despite Sanders' record-breaking double circumnavigation of the world four years earlier in *Perie Banou*. This time there would be no taking on supplies en route. Even this experienced yachtsman was challenged by the sheer logistics of surviving alone for almost two years.

An inventory of the required food and equipment to last the distance comprised an extraordinary three-and-a-half tonnes of stowage. Groceries, alone, weighed in at almost 2500 kilograms. These included

*End of the voyage... Jon Sanders' triumphant return to Fremantle at the end of his historic triple world circumnavigation.*

400 tins of baked beans, 300 packets of dried peas, five drums of salt, 50 jars of peanut butter, eight bottles of tomato sauce, 20 kg of cheese and 30 instant puddings. Vegemite? Yes, 50 jars of the Australian icon, too. Interestingly, the yachtsman also took aboard 15 dozen eggs, presumably fresh because they were first smeared with Vaseline, then wrapped individually in cling plastic. The scale of

required chandlery and hardware was equally demanding. It included eight spare plastic sextants, three yachtsman pocket knives, navigation rules, binoculars, six feet of chain, an assortment of 20 screwdrivers, four hacksaws and 30 hacksaw blades, 16 shifting spanners, 15 plastic buckets with wire handles (fitted one into the other), lots of various-sized self-tapping screws, nuts, bolts and washers, nine pairs of pliers and five dozen clothes pegs. All this food and gear, while only a small percentage of the overall inventory, give some idea of the necessities of life for such a long and lone voyage.

*Parry Endeavour* also carried an extensive ocean science package, including a specialised echo sounder and satellite transmitter and tracking system, installed by the Centre for Marine Science and Technology of WA's Curtin University. Acting as project managers, scientific staff could pinpoint his position daily, an invaluable asset particularly when Sanders lost radio contact for five months and they were still able to track his movements. The equipment also allowed the yachtsman to make scientific observations, such as recording surface temperatures and mapping sea mounds. In so doing he was able to confirm the existence of a major underwater land mass in the southern Pacific, where mountain peaks three kilometers high rose from the seabed five kilometers down. It was the first time such high-tech equipment had been installed on such a small vessel and the university was thrilled with the results. For Sanders it gave real purpose to a voyage of discovery, following in the footsteps of his hero Captain Cook (after whose ship, *Endeavour*, the sloop was renamed).

*Parry Endeavour* had left Fremantle on May 25, 1986, westward bound for the Cape of Good Hope. It was a stormy day, perhaps a small reminder of the unpredictability of what bigger things might lie ahead. The first circumnavigation took 249 days, after which Sanders turned his yacht about and headed east for the Horn. As the food diminished and the boat became progressively lighter, the last two laps were rather like running downhill, completed in 228 days and 178 days respectively.

The rest is history. When 48-year-old Jonathan William Sanders sailed into Fremantle on the morning of Sunday, March 13, 1988, he had travelled 71,023 nautical miles (131,535 kilometres) in 657 days, 21 hours and 18 minutes. He had set 15 records in the Guinness Book of Records and completed a huge, personal achievement as the longest non-stop solo voyager in history.

# Some Quay advice for early English girl migrants

## Victoria Quay
## Map Ref: 26

**A** **1927 handbook advised** young English women contemplating migrating to Western Australia: "We hope that not any of the English girls believe the yarns that when they arrive in Australia there is a bunch of roses waiting on the wharf for them, and a husband around the corner."

The pocket-size booklet was published by the Women's Immigration Auxiliary Council of Western Australia, which looked after migrant girls the moment they stepped ashore at Victoria Quay. The girls would be accommodated temporarily at the council's Fremantle centre before being sent as house-keepers to households in Perth or the country.

Today, the stretch of cargo sheds still in place diagonally opposite the E-Shed Markets is an almost silent reminder of the halcyon years of ship travel and the diverse periods of immigration, particularly in the "populate or perish" post-World War II period when hundreds of thousands of migrants came by ship to Australia. For many years Victoria Quay - which until Queen Victoria's death in 1901 had been known as South Quay - was the focal point of the mass movement of people coming and going. It was where Australian troops embarked for the battlefields of two world wars. It was where Royal visits began and ended, with the red carpet fanfare of the times. These were the days of the great international shipping lines, when giant liners pulled in to Victoria Quay about as regularly as taxis at a taxi rank.

So in 1927 when WA's population was just 377,000, the women's council was keen to encourage young women to come to Australia. The booklet - *A Word For Girl Migrants* - stated: "Those girls who have the spirit of travel and adventure cannot do better than turn their thoughts to Australia, where they will find their own kith and kin waiting to give them a very hearty welcome. Taking Western Australia generally, in both town and country districts, the girl most sought after is the girl with a general knowledge of house-keeping and who, even if she is not efficient on arrival, is willing and eager to learn; and who will take her share in helping the mother of the house in her manifold duties. . . . not only can they always obtain good situations, but it

*Orcades arriving at Victoria Quay.*

*The original Government Immigration Office, now called the Old Police Station and used as a shipping office.*

fits them to become useful wives and mothers, and so help us in our efforts to build up this immense country."

During this period British settlers had also been attracted to WA under the disastrous Group Settlement Scheme. The lure was the promise of free land to become farmers, carving out allocated allotments from virgin bush in the South-West. But lack of resources and farming skills, along with the primitive conditions took their toll and by 1924 a large percentage of the settlers had walked off the land.

The group settlers and the influx of young single women to WA are a microcosm of the overall, much larger picture of immigration which waxed and waned in make-up and volume many times over the years. In the post-war period numbers rose rapidly with the introduction of a new and large-scale migration program. Some 54,000 migrants came to WA between 1948 and 1954, leaving behind war-ravaged Europe for the promise of a better life "down under".

*After disembarkation in the post-war flood of migration.*

Between the end of World War 11 and 1975 more than three million migrants arrived in Australia, mostly via assisted passage schemes such as the £10 fare for accepted Britons, who earned the title of "ten pound Poms." Ultimately, the new face of Australia was to become a blend of nationalities from dozens of different countries. And Fremantle's Victoria Quay was the single gateway to the bulk of this incoming tide of people, for most their first landfall in Australia before disembarking either as new WA residents or as passengers in transit to eastern States capitals.

Many of the larger liners berthed at F Shed at the eastern end of the quay, but there was no fixed point for disembarkation. Many of the new arrivals would have sought information at the small weatherboard building facing the gap between C and D sheds, now known as the Old Police Station. Just down from the E Shed Markets, this building was the original Government Immigration Office and Information Bureau, built quayside in 1906 and shifted to its present location six years later.

The statue of C.Y. O'Connor was also positioned there, looking seawards above the heads of people streaming ashore after clearing Customs. While relocated to the western end of Victoria Quay in 1974, its earlier presence at the gateway of Australia's mass migration is a fitting reminder that, had other circumstances prevailed, Fremantle might never have been in a position to welcome a single migrant ship.

*The ships whose names once appeared in the daily arrival and departure lists of newspapers have long since gone to that great shipyard in the sky, memorable ghosts of a romantic age of travel. Names like* Orion, Orcades, Orontes, Orsova, Oronsay *and* Otranto, *the big O's of the Orient Line. Or, from the P and O group,* Himalaya, Strathaird, Stratheden, Strathmore *and* Strathnavar. *There was the Sitmar Line with its* Fairsea, Shaw Savill *with* Dominion Monarch *and* Southern Cross *and Lloyd Triestino's* Oceania, Australis *and* Neptunia.

*Then there were the vessels that plied the coastal and northern waters between capital cities - among them* Kanimbla, Duntroon, Manoora *and WA's own* Koolinda *- as well as those linking Fremantle with regular services to Singapore and Kuala Lumpur, like* Charon *and* Centaur.

*These were just some of the passenger ships that berthed regularly at Victoria Quay in the days before jet planes began making inroads into travel and migration. In a single year in the early 1950s, at least 40 passenger liners made 267 visits to Fremantle, some completing four trips from Europe in that time. Today, all of those ships, along with many others, have been scrapped. And the number of visits by passenger ships, now all cruise vessels, can almost be counted on one hand.*

# C.Y. O'Connor: Triumph to tragedy

O'Connor Memorial Statue
Victoria Quay
Map Ref: 27

**D**espite only living in Western Australia for 11 years, Irish-born civil engineer Charles Yelverton O'Connor had a profound and lasting impact on the State.

His two major achievements - Fremantle Harbour and the Perth to Kalgoorlie water pipeline - are as legendary as his death was tragic.

O'Connor was born in County Meath in 1843. At the age of 22 he emigrated to New Zealand to further his engineering career. O'Connor quickly built a reputation as a builder of railways and harbours and at the age of 48 had reached the position of Marine Engineer, responsible for the overall supervision of marine and public works in NZ.

He had married Susan Ness in 1874 and by the time a disagreement with the NZ Government prompted him to accept an offer from WA Premier Sir John Forrest to become WA's Engineer-in-Chief, there were seven children still living. Forrest had learned of O'Connor's reputation from a NZ delegate to the Australian Federal Convention of 1891. Replying to O'Connor's query as to what work the position entailed, Forrest replied: "Railways, harbours, everything." By the end of May, 1891, after 26 years in NZ, O'Connor was on his way to WA, then a colony on the brink of major expansion.

Described as slim, tall, erect, athletic and a man of cultivated tastes, he had wide interests and a lively wit. However, when angry he had a habit of jumping on his hat. This was an expensive foible because he had a big head and his hats had to be made in, then sent from, London.

O'Connor's first task in WA was to establish a long-awaited safe harbour at Fremantle. In November 1892 construction officially began when the wife of the Governor ceremonially started the building of the North Mole. Work was completed on schedule and the harbour was officially opened in May 1897 when Lady Forrest steered *SS Sultan* through the channel blasted from the limestone bar which had virtually blocked the river mouth.

Also in 1892, gold was discovered at Coolgardie and nine months later at Kalgoorlie. This sparked a huge population explosion in the arid Eastern Goldfields region. O'Connor, who was also in charge of railway expansion in WA, had been aware for some time of the inland water problem. This was now exacerbated by the gold rush. By the end of 1896 he had resigned his railways post to concentrate on other public works, the most important of which was the Goldfields water supply scheme. O'Connor's plan - to pump water from Mundaring more than 550km to the Goldfields - was bold and imaginative, too much so for many in the colony and he became the target of ill-informed and malicious public criticism. These attacks and the silence of the State Government (Forrest, his main supporter, had entered Federal Parliament at this stage) wounded O'Connor deeply. He was depressed, affected by ill-health and insomnia intensified by overwork and nervous exhaustion.

A fine horseman, it was O'Connor's habit to rise early each morning for a ride. On March 10, 1902 his usual companion, his youngest daughter Bridget, was ill so he went alone but not before leaving a note saying that the "position has become impossible...I feel my brain is suffering and I am in great fear of what effect all this worry may have upon me - I have lost control of my thoughts." He rode past the harbour, south to Robb Jetty and into the ocean. He dismounted, stood with his back to the waves and shot himself.

It was widely, but erroneously, said and taught for many years that O'Connor had committed suicide because water had not got to the Goldfields when he predicted and as a result he despaired, believed the scheme was a failure and took his own life. And according to Aboriginal legend O'Connor was 'sung' to death because by removing the limestone river bar he had damaged an ancient Aboriginal dreaming trail and could never be forgiven by the Bibbulmun people. Aboriginal clans affected by his action are said to have focused their negative energy on him, chanting a song that eventually caused him to take his life.

As O'Connor had forecast, the Goldfields scheme was completed successfully and officially opened in January 1903 with Forrest paying tribute to O'Connor as "the great builder of this work....to bring happiness and comfort to the people of the Goldfields for all time." In 1911 an impressive statue by Fremantle sculptor Pietro Porcelli was unveiled on Victoria Quay. Eighty eight years later a stylised 350kg bronze scupture by local artist Tony Jones, of O'Connor on horseback, was mounted in the water about 40m off the beach at the old Robb Jetty abattoir site.

O'Connor had strong links with WA's early horse-racing industry and was Fremantle's first hunt master. This link was carried on by his son-in-law and grandson, both Sir Ernest Lee-Steeres, who were both chairman of the WA Turf Club and prominent race-horse owners, winning several WA Derbies, Perth, Sydney and Caulfield Cups and a second to the legendary Phar Lap in the 1930 Melbourne Cup.

O'Connor's name lives on in WA with a Federal electorate, a suburb, a beach, a park, a ferry landing (Victoria Quay) and a Technical college named after him. His grave is in the Fremantle Cemetery, on the left-hand side of the driveway, 100m east of the main entrance.

*Left: The Pietro Porcelli statue at Fremantle Harbour.*
*Below: The bronze scuplture of O'Connor on horseback in the sea where he met his death.*

# The rock that barred a colony's mail

Fremantle Harbour
Victoria Quay
Map Ref: 26

An outcrop of limestone abutting the WA Maritime Museum at the western end of Victoria Quay is a visible reminder of the days before Fremantle had a proper harbour. The piece of rock was part of an original limestone bar that straddled the river from shore to shore, effectively preventing shipping from entering what is now Fremantle Inner Harbour.

All that changed in 1892 when the Forrest government agreed to follow the advice of the colony's engineer-in-chief, Charles Yelverton O'Connor. Despite earlier criticism of such a plan, he recommended the bar be removed and the river mouth developed as a harbour. The government's decision was a momentous one for the small but fast-developing colony. Within eight years, Western Australia had a fine port facility which has stood the test of time to this day.

It wasn't always so. From 1852 until the new harbour was completed, Fremantle was bypassed by the mail steamers from England. Instead, they used the natural deep port of Albany, 400 kilometres south, on their regular route to eastern ports. This may never have changed had the Premier, John Forrest, not recognised the value of building the port where his political support was strongest.

*The visible remains of the limestone bar abutting the WA Maritime Museum.*

To this day it is argued Fremantle's gain was Albany's loss.

Until the harbour was built, merchant ships mostly berthed alongside the unprotected Long Jetty off Bathers Beach. Their cargoes were then shifted along Cliff Street to the Swan River, from where they were ferried to Perth, itself a costlier exercise than the voyage from England. Built in 1872, Long Jetty was far from ideal, as Captain D.B. Shaw of the sailing ship *Saranac* noted in a report after arriving from New York in October 1892 . "It is a terrible place," he wrote unambiguously. "No place to put a vessel. No shelter whatever. All the ships have to lay and discharge at the wharf or pay lighterage. No place to send a ship of this size. Any man who would come or send a ship a second time is a damned ass."

It is not clear whether Shaw did return, but within a month of his departure for Launceston, work began on the construction of one of the two major breakwaters (now known as the North and South Moles). By 1894 there was sufficient weather protection to begin blasting and removing the bar - a not inconsiderable feat given available technology and the size and nature of the project. A year before it had been suggested tunneling beneath the bar and 'mining' the rock from above until it was ready to dynamite. Taking into account the porosity and questionable strength of the limestone, it is fortunate the idea was rejected and almost certain disaster averted.

*Thar she blows... blasting the bar.*

Instead, jarrah trestles were built to provide a stable footing on sections of the immersed rock. Long planks were added to form a basic platform for hand-drilling operations. The surface water above the rock varied from shallow to seven metres deep, and tidal changes also had to be considered. Boats were used to carry the trestles from place to place and as many as 160 men could be involved at any one time. Holes were drilled in the rock, packed with dynamite and exploded. Dredging plant brought from overseas was used inside and outside the bar to remove the shattered rock and, in September 1895, the bucket dredger *Fremantle* cut through the bar and moved into the river. Dredging work continued to deepen the harbour, while wharves were built on its northern and southern flanks, providing extensive parallel berthing and easy turnaround and movement for the biggest ships. Indeed, O'Connor was way ahead of his time with his parallel wharf design. Unlike other ports, including Sydney and Auckland where finger wharf harbours had been built as late as the 1920s,

Fremantle did not require major restructure to meet the changing needs of modern shipping.

Inner Harbour was officially opened by Lady Forrest in 1897, but it wasn't until 1900 that the first mail steamer from Britain came to Fremantle. The following year marked the first Royal visit - by the future King George V and Queen Mary - when Victoria Quay was officially named.

Since those early days, Fremantle Port has grown with the fortunes of the State, reflecting the time and tide of change and progress, the gateway for commerce and for people - for servicemen and women in two world wars, for many thousands of New Australians, for tourists and for travellers. Its functional capacity, even when chosen strategically as the largest wartime submarine base in the southern hemisphere, has never faltered.

On final analysis, its continued success is much due to the foreword thinking of an Irish engineer, and a limestone bar which, he insisted, should be removed.

# The day a vital wartime base almost blew up

Fremantle Harbour
North Quay
Map Ref: 28

**M**ost people gazing over Fremantle today would have no idea of the vital but little-known role the town and port played during World War II and the drama that threatened to bring it undone in 1945.

With the allied forces experiencing severe setbacks in Asian and Pacific regions during the war, Fremantle became a key strategic submarine base - the biggest in the southern hemisphere.

But that base - and the port - almost disappeared on January 17, 1945.

Just after 3pm on the 42 degree day, a fire broke out at No. 8 berth North Quay. It soon engulfed *MV Panamanian*, a merchant vessel loading flour, then quickly spread to the Royal Navy submarine depot ship, *HMS Maidstone*, which was loaded with torpedoes, ammunition and dieseline. With 20 loaded United States, British and Dutch submarines alongside depot ships in the port, there were fears that *Maidstone* would explode and the fire spread to other vessels. Fire-fighting efforts began immediately. *Maidstone* was towed away from the wharf and its fire extinguished.

The fire was eventually under control by daybreak on January 18. However, a strong easterly wind that day reignited the blaze and it was not until 5pm that control was restored and another six days before all the fire-fighting equipment was withdrawn. The fire had caused damage of more than $1 million to the wharf and *Panamanian* and claimed the life of a British seaman.

But most importantly the valuable work of the submarine fleet, which began with the arrival of *USS Holland* in March 1942, was able to continue.

*Wartime colours - the look of Victoria Quay as a strategic submarine base.*

By 1942 the Allied war effort in South-East Asia was in trouble. The major British base at Singapore had fallen to the Japanese, Pearl Harbour had been attacked and the United States driven out of its South Pacific bases. Northern Australian ports - including Broome and Wyndham in Western Australia - had been bombed by the Japanese and there were fears that Japan might continue its southward push and occupy part of the Australian mainland.

Between 1942 and 1945 Fremantle was host to more than 170 American, British and Dutch submarines which made more than 400 patrols out of the port. US boats stationed at Fremantle sank more Japanese oil tankers than all other US subs combined and made a significant contribution to total merchant vessel and warship sinkings. Two individual submarines based at Fremantle each sank more enemy shipping than any other allied sub in any theatre of war. The Fremantle-based submarines were also used to rescue civilians or servicemen trapped behind enemy lines or to land

and pick up commandos on Japanese-held islands north of Australia. Eleven US submarines were reported as sunk or lost out of Fremantle from a total of 123. An anti-submarine defence net system was installed at the harbour entrance and an elaborate boom defence system was installed in Cockburn Sound.

It has not been until relatively recently that Fremantle's vital strategic role in WWII has been properly recognised. Except for people living or working near the port little was known about the base. Security measures kept the submarines' activities away from wider public knowledge and the topic was generally ignored by Australian war historians because the RAN did not have any submarines of its own at the time.

However, the presence of the submariners in Fremantle was well-known to the local population. The US Navy took over 16 warehouses and a number of other buildings, including the former asylum and old women's home in Finnerty Street. New buildings were constructed on North Quay and by 1944 more than 200 civilian workers were employed directly in USN facilities. Many others were involved in providing support services. And a number of men from the submarines and submarine tenders met and married local girls.

The submariners' contribution is honoured by memorials on Monument Hill. The US Submariners' Association memorial was erected in 1967. Nearby is an unusual memorial which was unveiled in 1972 on the anniversary of the Battle of Trafalgar - the 14m, 1.25-tonne periscope from the British submarine *Tabard*. This was a gift from the RN to thank Fremantle for all it had done during the last war - and since - and commemorates the close ties forged between the people of Fremantle and the officers and men of the British and Allied submarines based in Fremantle during WWII.

*The Panamanian fire... when the Allied base - and the port - almost disappeared.*

# Pub meeting led to a lasting commercial success

Fremantle Chamber of Commerce
16 Phillimore Street
Map Ref: 30

**I**n his time, **Elias Solomon wore many hats.** He was variously Mayor of Fremantle, president of the Fremantle Tramways Board, chairman of the Hospital Board, the honorary WA Consul for Italy in Western Australia and an elected member of both State and Federal Parliaments, the first politician to represent Fremantle in the newly formed House of Representatives.

Clearly, he was a man of some influence. Indeed, it was he who formally proposed that a representative committee of Fremantle's merchants and business interests be formed, opening the way in 1873 to establish the Fremantle Chamber of Commerce, Australia's second oldest still in existence.

Solomon had migrated to Australia with his parents, living briefly in Sydney before moving to Adelaide in 1840 where he grew up and worked for an auctioneering firm. In 1866, then in his mid-twenties, he came to the West and entered business as an auctioneer and general merchant. Married twice and the father of five sons and four daughters, Elias Solomon remained in Western Australia for the rest of his life. He died in Fremantle on May 23, 1909.

Almost to the day 36 years earlier, on May 29, 1873 Solomon and other leading local merchants and residents had met at the Emerald Isle Hotel, a single storey building on the corner of High and Henry Streets where the Orient Hotel now stands. Most of the notable merchants of the day were present, including William D. Moore, William Marmion and John McGibbon who, along with Elias Solomon, were elected to a committee to formulate rules for a suitable Chamber. Just four days later, the committee met and the Fremantle Chamber of Commerce became a reality, quickly gathering momentum and a significant place in Fremantle society. W.D. Moore was its first president. Within four months, membership had grown to 40.

Copies of the Chamber's annual reports show that, in real terms, it became a force to be reckoned with in those early days of the developing colony. Taking over the reins of a representative WA Chamber of Commerce, which had floundered and closed after 20 years of disparate activity, the Fremantle body spread its influence beyond the port city as it saw fit to promote the commercial and economic benefits of the State.

Departmental bureaucracy was already alive and well by the turn of the century, as the reports of 1909/1910 show. During that year the Chamber

*Commerce in action... The Fremantle Chamber had a big influence on the development and operation of Fremantle Port.*

twice interceded on behalf of farmers and traders whose goods had been held up by Customs. In one instance, shipments of corn sacks were not allowed to be landed in WA because the sacks did not conform precisely to a standard weight. Following Chamber action and an approach to Premier John Forrest, the shipments, needed urgently by the State's farmers, were released almost immediately. In the same year the Chamber fought unimaginative quarantine rules to allow potatoes to be imported from Victoria to the goldfields and sorted out problems forbidding the landing of jute goods from Calcutta.

Clearly the Chamber's actions went beyond local merchants' immediate concerns to take in the broader State perspective. Gambling in the booming goldfields and its effect on trade prompted the resolution - "that this Chamber strongly condemns the excessive gambling which obtains on the goldfields and applauds the action of the business people at Kalgoorlie and Boulder in waiting upon the acting-Premier (Mr Wilson) with a request that the Government enforce the anti-gambling laws of this State. . ."

Closer to home, the Chamber had already been a major player in matters concerning the very establishment of the Port of Fremantle and its associated infrastructure and facilities. It took a strong stand against excessive government port charges, and worked to streamline shipping paperwork. It had a critical role in lobbying for

Fremantle to become the preferred mail port to Albany and in the movement of cargoes by river barge from Fremantle to Perth. When the Fremantle Harbour Trust was formed in 1902, some of the Chamber members became commissioners to assist with the control of all the wharves and harbours and the berthage of ships and cargo distribution.

It wasn't until 1912 that the Chamber gained its prominent, physical presence in the stately building at 16 Phillimore Street from which it has operated ever since. The site became available after the Perth railway station shifted from its original location nearby in 1907. From its new premises the Chamber continued its strong association with the Port and shipping. Later it also had to address serious new problems emerging from the Great Depression and the difficult times of two world wars.

Today, with a membership of more than 450 companies and individuals, its scope has widened to the forceful promotion of Fremantle's commercial activity - and the equally strong defence of its unique position as the historical heart of WA. What has not changed is the original intent of the motion moved by Elias Solomon in 1873 - to establish "some combination for active united concert to protect and advance the interest of trade."

# Fremantle rail link survives a chequered past

Fremantle Railway Station
Elder Place
Map Ref: 31

*This was the scene outside Fremantle Railway Station in 1924 when a large crowd gathered to watch men of the Special Service Squadron entraining for a march through Perth.*

**E**arly on Easter Monday, April 18, 1892, a special train left Fremantle for the inland town of York and a big day at the races. The train was pulled by two steam engines, the first of which, No 29, was driven by 32-year-old Harry Wright. A native of Birmingham, Wright had been in the colony for just five years and was one of the most popular and keen drivers on the line. On this Easter occasion he had decided to wear the brand new cap given him by his wife, Alice. It was a fateful decision. As the train began its river crossing, a gust of wind blew his cap off and, reaching out to grab it, his wrist hit against a cross-piece of a telephone pole. The impact threw him off balance and he fell from the train to the bridge, hitting his head against the engine in the process. Despite the best efforts of the train crew to revive him, Wright died soon after, the train resuming its journey after a 15-minute delay. Subsequently, flags were flown at half-mast on most Fremantle public buildings and a subscription was raised for Wright's widow and her four children.

The tragic story of Harry Wright is part of the chequered history of the oldest stretch of railway still operating in Western Australia, itself a story of survival. It began in the late 1870s when more efficient transportation became a necessity between the port and Perth. Since 1836, river ferry had been the main means of transport. Now a rail link was the logical solution.

It took two years to build the railway from Fremantle via Perth to Guildford, including the first railway bridge, and a day of congratulatory speeches from all and sundry to officially open it. In fact, on

March 1, 1881, the Governor, Sir William Robinson, declared the line open three times - first in Fremantle, then in Guildford and finally in Perth - and promised that the so-called Eastern Railway would soon be extended to York. It was a Tuesday morning when the governor was escorted by a military guard of honour to the Perth station, where he and dignitaries boarded the special train, decorated with flags and greenery, to make the 26-minute journey to Fremantle.

Fremantle welcomed the governor with a prophetic speech from the chairman of the Municipal Council, Mr Elias Solomon, who said, "we look upon this event as the dawn of a new era in the history of the colony." His words were soon confirmed by the dramatic expansion of the rail system, which included extending the line further eastwards to York and Kalgoorlie, as well as to the safe waters of South Beach and Robb's Jetty, where thousands of people flocked for weekends and holidays. Ironically, the boom in railway traffic ultimately worked against the best interests of Fremantle where, in 1886, the first railway workshops had been built - despite political pressure to have them located in Perth. As it turned out, the huge increase in rolling-stock needing repair and maintenance was too much for the workshops to handle in an area which became increasingly congested. At any one time as many as 400 wagons could be waiting for attention. So despite continuing efforts to improve facilities, in 1904 the workshops were shifted to Midland, east of Perth. As well as the loss of an important activity, the change meant the transfer of several hundred workmen to Midland. Initially, they remained in Fremantle and caught the train to work. With cycling becoming a popular

sport, many would even race the train from Fremantle to Midland as part of their training. However, in time the bulk of the 700 workers shifted home, causing a noticeable downturn in the Fremantle population.

With the closure of the Fremantle workshops, the original station in Phillimore Street was shut down and a new one built where it stands today. The new station was opened in 1907 and, apart from the later demolition of a platform and parcels office, remains structurally unchanged. In 1979, the State Government decided to close the passenger service because of declining patronage with no perceived prospects for growth. The decision was another retrograde one for Fremantle but, happily, one that was reversed in 1983 when, after vigorous public outcry, a new government chose to restore the service. Since then, the rail service has progressed steadily. The passenger service which began with six trains a day in 1882, not unexpectedly, now operates day and night with average weekly boardings exceeding 156,000.

Whether tourists, school groups, or local people having a day out, many use the service to visit Fremantle, passing beneath the station's arched roof with its swans perched decoratively atop, as they have done for almost a hundred years.

# Heroism honoured at Army Museum

WA Army Museum
Artillery Barracks, Burt Street
Map Ref: 33

*Frederick Bell VC*

**T**he concise, almost bland citation which records the battlefield heroics of Frederick Bell - the first West Australian to win the Victoria Cross - gives only a fleeting clue to his astonishing life which later included being mauled by a lion.

In May, 1901, during the Boer War in South Africa, Bell's unit was involved in a skirmish with a big group of Boers who had sprung a trap at Brakpan, in Transvaal.

Bell, then a Lieutenant, was ordered to hold a position at the edge of a stream until the rest of the company could get to safety. With the task accomplished and about to move on, Bell noticed a horse fall in front of him and went to the rider's assistance. Bell's commanding officer, Captain John Campbell, rode over to help but as they got the man on Bell's horse it fell under the extra weight. Bell told Campbell and the man to ride off while he positioned himself behind an anthill and started firing at the fast-approaching Boers. When the main Australian group reached high ground Bell was able to rejoin them under their covering fire.

The citation and replicas of the 10 medals Bell received for his services to the British Empire are featured in the WA Army Museum, generally regarded as the best military museum outside Canberra, the home of the Australian War Memorial.

Bell was born in Perth in 1875. In 1894 he joined the Colonial WA Customs service and worked there until the outbreak of the Boer War in 1899 when he enlisted as a Private in the 1st West Australian (Mounted Infantry) Contingent. He fought in several major engagements, was seriously wounded in 1900 and invalided to England. After a partial recovery he returned to WA. Still not fit, he bluffed his way through another medical examination, returned to South Africa with the 6th (Mounted Infantry) Contingent and subsequently won the VC, the highest Commonwealth decoration for heroism in combat.

Life in Africa obviously appealed to Bell and he left WA in 1905 and joined the British Colonial Office. His well-known skill as a big game hunter was sorely tested in British Somaliland in 1909 when he was charged by a lion. He shot it, but managed only to infuriate it by blowing away its lower jaw. The lion and Bell wrestled in the dust until help arrived. His body was ripped open, a lung collapsed and his skull injured and he spent six months in England recovering. During World War I Bell served as an officer in the British Army, was wounded again and finished as the Commandant of the Embarkation Camps in Plymouth with the rank of Lieut-Colonel.

Bell resumed his career with the Colonial Service in Africa as a Political Officer until he retired in 1925. He then returned to the United Kingdom where he remained until he died in 1954. He is buried in Canford Cemetery, Bristol. His VC has special significance. Although other West Australians subsequently won the VC, Bell's was the only one awarded to a soldier fighting under the West Australian flag (before the formation of the Australian Army in 1901).

*World War II display depicting a jungle operating theatre for Australian prisoners.*

Bell's medals were bought by the WA Museum for $48,000 in 1984. The Army Museum is located at Artillery Barracks, established on Cantonment Hill in two phases between 1910 and 1913. It holds four original VCs, including one awarded in the Afghanistan War in 1880, and the replica medal groups of all WA VC recipients - either born in WA or who won the medal with a WA unit. The Museum has the biggest collection of VCs in Australia outside the Australian War Memorial.

The Museum, established in 1977 and originally located in East Perth, moved to Fremantle in 1995 and includes a pre-1914 gallery, a reconstructed WWI trench, a WWI gallery, a graphic life-sized Prisoner of War gallery, a WWII gallery and a post-1945 gallery. The parade ground in front of the museum has a collection of vehicles, tanks and artillery.

The Museum collection tells the story of WA army service from the Colonial era to the present. One of the many interesting or unusual items on display is a sleeveless pullover knitted by a WA soldier serving in 11th Battalion who was captured during WWI. The soldier unravelled parcels of woollen socks sent to the German POW camp and knitted the pullover with needles fashioned from camp fence wire.

The Museum shares the Barracks - the oldest commissioned barracks in continuous use in WA-with the Army Reserve unit, the WA University Regiment. The site was chosen because of its elevated position near the river. However, the decision did not please everyone because the land on the top of the hill was a popular picnic spot.

And while the Museum's future is now assured it was not always so. In 2000 the Museum faced the prospect of have to move again because of Federal Government plans to sell the site. A "Save the Barracks" campaign was initiated and after lengthy negotiations the Commonwealth agreed to allow the Museum to stay under special licensing arrangements.

The 3.8ha site is heritage listed on the National Estate Register. The Museum is supported by two Army Reserve Officers (manager and curator) and about 80 volunteers and 120 sponsor members. It is open to the public from 11am-3pm on Wednesdays and between 12.30 and 4.30pm on Saturdays and Sundays. During school holiday periods it is open every day between 10am and 4pm. School and group tours can be arranged outside advertised hours by appointment. During school holiday periods it is open every day between 10am and 4pm.

# Pioneer church honoured by the Pope

St Patrick's Basilica
W.E. Marmion Celtic Cross
Proclamation Tree
Adelaide Street
Map Ref: 34

**St Patrick's Basilica** - one of only five Roman Catholic churches in Australia to be accorded this honour - has played a pivotal role in Fremantle's social history.

The Papal symbol of crossed keys set over the entrance to the Basilica demonstrates its special status - a long way from the church's beginnings on flood-prone land near the Fremantle foreshore.

By the early 1840s local Catholics had become worried by increasing Protestant activity in Fremantle. In December 1841 Catholic layman Robert D'Arcy wrote to the Church in Sydney requesting a priest be sent to the fledgling Swan River Colony to counter the activities of the Anglicans and Methodists. The Anglicans had a particularly vigorous Minister, George King, who by 1843 - two years after his arrival - had overseen the building of the first St John's Anglican Church in a prominent position in High Street.

Persuaded that action was necessary, the Catholic hierarchy appointed Irish-born Father John Brady, then pastor of the Windsor area near Sydney, to take charge of the Catholic mission in WA. Ahead of his arrival in WA in December 1843 local Catholics

obtained permission from the Governor to hold Sunday services in the local courthouse at the bottom of High Street near the Round House.

In 1847, Brady, by then Bishop of Perth, bought land in Henry Street and a room in a cottage on the property was used for Sunday mass. The introduction of convict labour in 1850 to speed up development in the Colony also helped the church. In 1852 Spanish Bishop Joseph Serra had a timber church, recorded as "The Church of St. Patrick, in the town of Fremantle," constructed next to the cottage. However, the Henry Street block was prone to ocean flooding and a more suitable site was sought - and found when the Church was granted land bound by Adelaide and Parry Streets.

A new St Patrick's was completed on the site in 1860, drawing praise three years later from Mrs Edward Millett, the wife of a visiting Anglican Minister, who wrote that the "Anglican Church (St John's) could not lay much claim to beauty either externally or within.....The Roman Catholics possess a much prettier and ecclesiastical building and their convent and clergy-house are neat and tidy buildings."

By 1891 about a third of Fremantle's growing population were Catholic and with the appointment of the Oblates of Mary Immaculate to the Fremantle parish in 1894 moves for a bigger and more suitable place of worship began. At a meeting in 1895 Bishop Matthew Gibney was applauded when he said: "The time has now come for Fremantle to have one of the best churches in the Colony." Prominent popular merchant and politician and leading lay supporter of the Church, William Marmion, moved that a new church was urgently needed. The motion was carried unanimously.

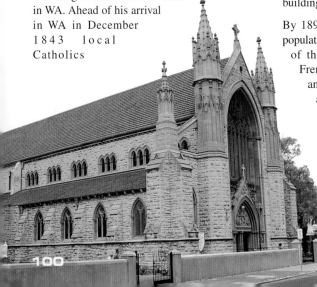

Sadly, Marmion did not see work on the new church begin. Born in Fremantle in 1845, he was the first Catholic to become a WA Cabinet Minister. His career in public life began at the early age of 23 when he became a member of the Fremantle Town Trust and soon after the first chairman of Fremantle's inaugural municipal council. A member of State Parliament at the age of 25 he developed extensive business interests including involvement in the pastoral, pearling, mining and maritime industries.

With the advent of self-government in WA and the formation of the Forrest Ministry in 1890, Marmion became the State's first Minister for Lands and Mines and was a WA delegate to the 1891conference in Sydney which discussed the formation of an Australian Commonwealth. His sudden death in 1896 at the age of 51 was a blow to the Fremantle Catholic and business communities and there was widespread support when a memorial was suggested. Fremantle sculptor Pietro Porcelli was commissioned to create an unusual, large, Celtic Cross memorial which was placed close to St Patrick's and the Moreton Bay fig tree which marks the proclamation of WA as a self-governing colony.

By the time the memorial was unveiled by Marmion's old friend, former Premier Sir John Forrest, in January 1902, the first stage of the new church had been completed. In late 1895 architects Michael and James Cavanagh had been commissioned to design the new church. The substantial structure, in the Federation Gothic style, was officially opened in June 1900 to huge fanfare. Special trains ran from Perth to bring people to the event. However, Michael Cavanagh's plans had not been fully implemented and efforts to complete the church were thwarted by difficult economic conditions and the outbreak of two World Wars.

It was not until 1955 that a concerted push to finish the building program bore fruit. That year saw the demise of the original church on the site, used as a hall since 1900. A fund-raising auction conducted by the Mayor W.F. (later Sir Frederick) Samson was the last big occasion held in the 95-year-old building. Work on Michael Cavanagh's church, now heritage-listed, was completed in 1959-60. Cavanagh, who had arrived in WA from South Australia in 1895, designed numerous commercial, civic, residential and ecclesiastical buildings in WA over a period of 40 years, including a new St Patrick's Presbytery, Christian Brothers' College in Perth, St. Brigid's Convent in Northbridge and the P and O Hotel, Hotel Orient and the Fire Station in Fremantle. He headed the design team for Aquinas College in the 1930s and died in 1941 at the age of 80.

*The Celtic Cross memorial and inscription, placed near the so-called Proclamation Tree.*

In 1994, coinciding with the centenary of the arrival of the Oblates - an order founded by Bishop Eugene de Mazenod in 1826 - a Papal decree conferred a rare honour on St Patrick's by granting it the status of a minor Basilica - an honorary title accorded because of a church's religious or historical importance. There are only four other basilicas in Australia - three in Victoria and one in Sydney.

# Bridges' vital link to capital and beyond

Fremantle traffic and railway bridges and Stirling Bridge
Map Ref: 35

**T**he establishment of the **Swan River Colony's** capital city, Perth, 19km upstream on the opposite side of the Swan River to Fremantle, caused transport problems between the Colony's two major settlements. Yet the only substantial bridge built in the Colony in the first 14 years of settlement was not at Fremantle but across the Helena River at Guildford, more than 30km away.

When the first settlers arrived in June 1829 land was opened for selection along both banks of the

Swan River. Settlements were also planned along both banks of the Canning River and it became obvious that bridges were needed for development. But they were slow coming.

In the early years transport was mainly via river barges though there were land routes along the southern and northern banks of the river. By 1834 there was a sandy bush track to Perth and runners carried the mail. At Claremont the Fremantle and Perth runners met and exchanged their bundles. The lack of a bridge had tragic consequences in 1830 for a doctor and a friend who tried to ferry a live cow across the river at Preston Point, East Fremantle, in a small boat. Not surprisingly, the boat capsized and both men drowned.

By 1849 bridges had been built over the Swan River Causeway in Perth and the Canning River, improving road access to Perth. But at Fremantle, the river was still a barrier. To the left of the current traffic bridge a capstan worked by convict labour dragged passengers and vehicles across in a big punt. It was not until 1863 - 34 years after settlement - that work began on the first bridge at Fremantle, built by convicts, including prisoners in chain gangs, mainly blasting and quarrying stone for the bridge approaches. One early report said: "Hundreds of men were engaged, working on punts, on the decking or on scaffolding. Warders with rifles were numerous and escape was practically impossible. Nevertheless escapes were attempted and there are dark legends of men having been shot down (during construction). Official records, however, show the loss of only one life, that of a convict who lost his hold on the bridge and fell into the river."

The bridge, completed in 1867, had 319 solid jarrah timber piles and a hump to allow the masts of sailing vessels to pass under. The 285m structure became known as the Stick Bridge and an English visitor in 1896 said it resembled a huge centipede. It was opened without official fanfare in 1866 but not before legendary horse-thief and gaol escapee Joseph

*Above: The "Stick Bridge" pictured in the 1880s. Built in 1867, it provided Fremantle-Perth access for 80 years.*

*Below: Crowds take in the drama after the railway bridge collapsed from heavy flooding in 1926.*

Johns, better known as Moondyne Joe, upstaged Governor John Hampton. On the night before the unpopular Hampton was to make the first crossing Johns broke out of gaol and cheekily scurried over the bridge to temporary freedom.

The bridge gave Fremantle better land access to Perth and facilitated the settlement of North Fremantle and Mosman Park but by the early 1890s its safety was being questioned. A notice in the Government Gazette in 1896 declared that *"until further notice, no person or persons shall be permitted to drive or lead any mob of cattle, camels or horses exceeding four in number over along or across this bridge..."*

By 1898 the bridge was considered unsafe and a low-level traffic bridge erected alongside. The new bridge was intended to be temporary while the original bridge was replaced by a wider structure. However, when the tramway was to be extended to North Fremantle it was decided that the lower bridge was at the wrong level. The original bridge was found to be in a generally sound condition and it was decided to renovate it. The hump was removed and the structure widened to allow road traffic as well as trams. It was used for another 30 years until replaced by the current traffic bridge in 1939 and demolished in 1947. The low-level bridge was closed in 1909 but used by fishermen until about 1920 when it was demolished and some of its wood turned into furniture for the North Fremantle Council chambers.

The second crossing at Fremantle was the railway bridge built downstream from the Stick Bridge in 1881. There was drama in April 1892 when train driver Harry Wright was killed in a tragic accident, trying to retrieve a cap that had blown off his head. He lost his balance and fell onto the bridge, dying soon afterwards. There was drama of

a different kind in July 1926 when the bridge collapsed - "smashed by floodwaters racing to the sea" - only moments after a train had crossed over. Abnormally heavy rains also washed away about 30m of riverbank. Railway gangs immediately stopped any following trains and "prevented a grand disaster from occurring." The bridge was under repair for the next three months, inconveniencing businesses and train travellers.

A new railway bridge was opened in 1964, close to the current traffic bridge which was built almost on the site of the 1898 temporary, low-level bridge. This bridge has had extensive renovations over the years, some not without controversy. Some of the work in a $13 million program in 1992 was described as a bungled, half-hearted attempt to restore the bridge's former character. The most recent Fremantle bridge - the Stirling Bridge - was built without fuss or controversy about 400m upstream and opened in 1974. The $3.4 million 415m long bridge connects Stirling and Canning Highways.

The Fremantle road and railway bridges had another use on Bloody Sunday in 1919. As Premier Hal Colebatch and his party passed under on their way to a confrontation with lumpers on Victoria Quay, angry demonstrators rained large stones, road metal and scrap iron onto the passing launches. The occupants escaped injury but several had miraculous escapes.

# The building with a haunted past

Fremantle Museum and Arts Centre
Corner Ord & Finnerty Streets
Map Ref: 36

*Fremantle Asylum in 1897.*

**W**hile music lovers enjoy free concerts in the open courtyard of the Fremantle Museum and Arts Centre, the ghosts of years gone by must look on with envy. This fine, neo-Gothic building which offers so much pleasure to visitors today, was once the darkest of places, its limestone walls enclosing a forbidding centre for decades of human suffering and sadness.

The building was purpose-built in 1861-64 as a lunatic asylum, its original design brought from England by Comptroller of Convicts Edmund Henderson on his second stint in Fremantle. The colony needed somewhere to properly accommodate those considered mentally unfit, whose temporary quarters until then were in a scatter of buildings on the site now occupied by the Esplanade Hotel.

Sadly, the word "lunatic" was defined conveniently to group together patients and prisoners in an overcrowded, under-serviced human melting pot, run strictly along prison lines. So-called colonial lunatics (local), imperial lunatics (convicts) and criminal lunatics (prisoners) were classified as either quiet and chronic, or maniacal and dangerous, melancholic and suicidal, idiotic, paralytic and epileptic. Records show that in 1903, a total 257 men and 108 women were patients in an asylum considered adequate enough for no more than 100 people. It took the murder of a woman inmate to prompt an official enquiry

which ultimately brought about the closure of the asylum in 1909.

For the next 30 years the building served simultaneously as a home for elderly women, a midwifery training school and what amounted to a detention centre for prostitutes. There were numerous interior building changes, but the facility progressively declined until it was closed.

In 1942 soon after the women were transferred elsewhere, the US navy moved in, using the centre to complement their naval base operations headquartered in the West End. While it housed guns and ammunition, trucks and other military equipment, its main use was for accommodating personnel in temporary barracks built in the centre's grounds.

At the end of World War II, the building was used variously for educational purposes, such as night tech classes and as an annexe for overcrowded local schools. In 1957, government authorities condemned it, immediately sparking calls for its restoration and preservation. Due in part to the intervention of Lord Mayor Sir Frederick Samson, the building was saved. Restoration began in 1968, followed by the opening of the Maritime Museum in 1970 and, in the following year, the Fremantle Arts Centre. The Fremantle History Museum was established when the Maritime Museum was relocated in the mid-1980s.

Not unexpectedly, ghost stories abound, with numerous recorded reports of people experiencing strange feelings while in certain areas of the old asylum building. Some have occurred during building alterations. Others, such as unexplained, sudden drops in room temperatures and odd sightings, have been recorded during visiting hours. Perhaps most common among these is the widely reported vision of a lady in black - supposedly either a mental patient or an inmate of the women's home.

In 1986, six psychics spent the night in the Fremantle Museum conducting an experiment in Extra Sensory Perception (ESP). They experienced feelings of agitation, the aura of death, fear and hostility. A member of the group summed it up as "a lot of conflicting atmosphere," adding that "people should not be afraid. There's nothing that's likely to harm them."

If, indeed, there are ghosts, their envy is understandable.

# Monument Hill - rising from barren waste

Corner of High and Swanbourne Streets
Map Ref: 37

**W**hen the first European settlers arrived at Fremantle, what is now Monument Hill was a rocky, barren, limestone outcrop with low scrub. But it had one thing in its favour - it had the best views in Fremantle and it was the most prominent landmark for shipping approaching the port.

With panoramic 360-degree views it has been a popular lookout and recreational area for Fremantle locals and visitors since European settlement. In 1907 The Morning Herald newspaper reported that "the outlook is appreciated by all visitors. It is in the evening, however, when the sun sinks beneath the horizon of the western ocean that Monument Hill is really appreciated by residents and visitors alike. Whichever direction the breeze may come from, it always blows cool across Monument Hill and at the close of the hottest day a half-hour spent on this resort will prove to be truly invigorating."

Today, that still applies although the site - and its use - has changed much over the years.

It was first put to use with the erection in 1867 of a stone obelisk as a navigational aid for shipping. The discovery of gold caused a population boom in Western Australia and although most immigrants passing through Fremantle went on to the goldfields, many stayed to find work. Few could be accommodated in the town so canvas 'towns' developed at various places including the Hill. This led to the removal of existing vegetation which was used for firewood and other purposes.

By 1897 the outcrop, one of Fremantle's 'Seven Hills', had become known as Monument Hill, and in 1904 the 11-acre site was vested in the city. In 1919 a prominent Fremantle businessman, Mr J.W. Bateman, asked the council to consider erecting a suitable and lasting memorial to Fremantle residents who had died during World War I. Two years later a citizens' deputation suggested that the obelisk be replaced by a memorial and the unkempt area beautified.

Designs for a war memorial were called for in 1922 but controversy involving the original design and fund-raising problems caused long delays. It was not until 1927, three years after the obelisk was demolished, that a local architectural firm, Allen and Nicholas, was appointed to modify the existing plan in light of the available funds. In the difficult financial environment of the time the public was less than enthusiastic about donating money for the project and

*Anzac Day, 1939*

collection tins were even handed around on the day of the unveiling ceremony.

metre memorial, constructed of Donnybrook stone at a cost of almost six thousand pounds ($12,000) - almost two thirds raised from public donations and the rest provided by the council - was finally completed in 1928. It was dedicated by the Governor, Sir William Campion, on Anzac Day and unveiled on Armistice Day. During the 1930s Depression sustenance workers laid lawns and established attractive garden beds. In 1961 stone pillars carrying plaques honouring those who died in World War II were erected.

It was the first significant war memorial erected in WA and is one of three major memorials in the State along with the State War Memorial in Kings Park, Perth, and the Desert Mounted Corps Memorial on Mt. Clarence, Albany.

Once built the memorial became a target for vandals and other mischief-makers. In 1932 there were complaints that it was being used as a two-up (gambling) school. The following year a Norfolk Island pine tree was destroyed, 500 petunia seedlings were stolen and the head gardener reported that empty beer bottles had to be removed regularly from the memorial.

During WWII there were complaints about servicemen stationed at the gun posts on the hill playing football. In July 1942 the council wrote to their commanding officer: "We respectfully suggest that this practice be stopped as such sport is inconsistent with the sentiments which are associated with a memorial of this nature and is tending to bring one of our admired reserves in disrepute."

The suggestion was ignored. Things came to a head in October 1943 when it was reported that the men were now using the memorial as a cricket wicket. Another strongly-worded letter from the council led to the men being reprimanded. Graffiti and vandalism were a problem in the 1980s and in the late 1990s the memorial was being damaged by skateboarders.

Monument Hill, which was placed on the Heritage Register in 2001, is now home to 11 memorials, three memorial gateways and several memorial plaques. Since 1928 the other memorials have been added to commemorate service personnel and operations in many different theatres of war.

# Moondyne Joe made a mockery of prison

**I**f Joseph Johns was alive today, he would probably be making a fortune as a professional escapologist. However, his final resting place in Fremantle Cemetery overrides fanciful conjecture with the fact that, however clever he was, the inevitable was inescapable.

The faded inscription on the tombstone also identifies the lesser known Johns as the better known Moondyne Joe, a name that stuck because of his many activities in the extensive region north of the Avon River known to the Aborigines as "Moondyne". Indeed, the tombstone is one of two lasting memorials - the other a much visited cell at Fremantle Prison where, over the years, Moondyne spent rather less time than his gaolers would have wished.

Joe came to Fremantle on a convict ship in 1853, having already served part of a 10-year prison sentence. He had been arrested in Monmouth, Wales, for stealing food. Two years after his arrival, he was granted conditional freedom. He soon headed east for the Toodyay district 50 kms from Perth where he scratched out a living in the bush rounding up stray stock, including horses, and returning them to their owners. Under the law, any unbranded horses of breeding

*Moondyne Joe, a rare photograph by Alfred Choppin.*

found this way had to be reported. However, Moondyne chose to ignore this and, instead, burned his own brand onto a half-bred stallion which led to his arrest in 1861 charged with horse stealing. That night he escaped from the Toodyay police lock-up, throwing the resident magistrate's saddle and bridle onto the horse he was accused of stealing and riding off. He later shot the horse and cut off the branding, removing any evidence to support the horse stealing charge. So when caught several days later, he was charged with the far less serious offence of prison breaking, for which he served three years in gaol without incident. Several months after his release in 1864, however, he was charged with killing a farmer's ox and sentenced to 10 years' gaol. In August 1866, he made his first dramatic escape over the prison walls - after somehow working his way from a cell where he had been shackled in leg-irons.

*Top: Moondyne Joe's grave. Left: Heritage Trail, Fremantle Cemetery. Right: Bon Scott's memorial seat.*

This time when recaptured, the authorities decided to make an example of Moondyne who, by now, had achieved something of a hero status. He was locked in leg-irons once more in a supposedly "escape-proof" cell and given nothing but bread and water. It was only in March 1867 after his health had deteriorated and the prison doctors recommended that he be given fresh air that he was allowed out to break stones in the prison yard, under strict guard. Amazingly, he managed to escape again, by hammering a hole through the prison wall while supposedly breaking rocks, the growing rock pile screening the guard's view. All that was found were Moondyne's outer garments - his coat balanced on an upright sledgehammer, the arms held out by piano wire - while the prisoner had fled in his flannel underwear.

This was not the finish of the Moondyne Joe saga. He remained free for two years before being caught helping himself to samples of the best at Houghtons winery. This time he was able to serve out the rest of his sentence under more lenient prison governance. Apart from a short period in the Perth lock-up in 1887 and a month in Fremantle Prison shortly before his death in 1900, he managed to stay out of trouble.

Moondyne is one of many recognisable names of the past whose epitaphs are scattered through the extensive acreage of Fremantle Cemetery. When the earlier cemeteries in Skinner Street and Alma Street made way for change and development, some

80 headstones were moved to Carrington Street, as were all discovered remains.

A walk through Heritage Trail brings the past alive. Names inscribed on monuments of many shapes and sizes leap from the history books - names like C.Y. O'Connor and Lionel Samson and John and Walter Bateman. Not far away from the trail is the small headstone of Ronald Belford Scott, alias Bon Scott, lead singer of the Australian AC/DC rock group. Bon Scott grew up in Fremantle and was educated at John Curtin High School. The memory of his short but turbulent life remains strong among fans and, since his death in 1980, his is the most visited site in the Fremantle Cemetery.

This is a place where the famous and the infamous, the rich and the poor, poets, politicians, prison warders and prisoners all come together, at last equal in their final resting place. Maybe for Moondyne Joe, this was his biggest escape after all.

# ACKNOWLEDGEMENTS

There are many people to thank for making available their time and knowledge in the preparation of this publication. While not a big book physically, the degree of research needed to cover the 50 separate subjects properly was very demanding. We sought the help of many authoritative sources as well as descendants and relatives of some of the subjects of this book. Many hours were spent in the local history section of the Fremantle City Library where, without the unstinting help of the ladies in charge, this book might not have seen the light of day. We would also like to acknowledge the assistance received from various people at the WA Maritime Museum, Fremantle Prison, Fremantle Ports and the University of Notre Dame. We hope we have not left out anyone in the following:

Alison Bauer, Loretta O'Reilly, Larraine Stevens, Fremantle City Library (Local History Collection); Jack Edwards; Margaret McPherson, oral historian; Samantha Torrens, Public Transport Authority; John Murdoch, Fremantle Markets Pty. Ltd; Brian Solosy, archivist, Jennifer Lane, secretary, Parish of St John's, Fremantle; Mike Lefroy, Head of Education, WA Maritime Museum; Terry Craig, Campus Services Manager, Carol Eaton, Senior Admin. Officer (Campus Services), Marcus Collins, architect, University of Notre Dame; Brian Goodall, Briten Security; Ainslie de Vos, Tim Walton, Alan Pearce, Belinda Ingram, Fremantle Ports; Graeme Gammie, Executive Manager, Rob Besford, Curatorial Assistant, Fremantle Prison; Norm Wrightson; Richard Maroney, Sail & Anchor; Alec Smith, Fremantle guide & historian; Nunzio Gumina, Limoncello Café; Ian Elliot, author *Moondyne Joe - The Man and the Myth*; Baden Pratt, Manager, Public Relations, Fremantle Hospital; Richard Moore, author *The Moores of Derry and Oakover*; Geoff Moore, W.D. Moore & Co; Ric McCracken, UnionsWA; Sally R. May, Head of Maritime History Department, Jeremy Green, Head of Department of Maritime Archaeology and Graeme Henderson, Director, WA Maritime Museum; Claude Basile; Brendan Woods, historian and *Catalpa* fanatic; Des Lambert, Tony Samson, Richard Erskine, Managing Director Lionel Samson and Son Pty Ltd; Peter Shaw and Wayne Gardiner, Curator, Army Museum of WA; John Blake; Barry Strickland; Stephen de Silva, Librarian, Main Roads WA; Karen Jardine, WA Regional History Officer, Australian Customs Service; Derek Pedley; Greg Nannup; Michael Culley, Culley's Tea Rooms; Vic Jeffrey, Defence Public Affairs (WA).

# ILLUSTRATIONS

With the exception of those listed below or acknowledged separately elsewhere, all black-and-white photographs are reproduced courtesy the Fremantle City Library (Local History Collection).

# BIBLIOGRAPHY

Warders and Gaolers: A Dictionary of Western Australian Prison Officers 1829-1870, compiled by David J Barker, WA Genealogical Society Inc.(2000): Hotels in Fremantle from the turn of the century - 1930. A living heritage, by Jill James (1984); FREO: A portrait of the port city, By Stan Gervas (1996); Moondyne Joe, The Man and the Myth, by Ian Elliot (1978); Fremantle Hospital - A Social History to 1987, by Phyl Garrick and Chris Jeffery (1987); The Moores of Derry and Oakover, by Richard K. Moore (2003); The Italian Fishermen of Fremantle, by Sally May (Journal of the Fremantle History Society); The Beginning: European Discovery and Early Settlement of Swan River Western Australia, by R.T. Appleyard and Toby Manford (1979); Westralian Portraits, Lyall Hunt, Editor (1979); C.Y. O'Connor; His Life and Legacy, by A.G. Evans (2001); Big John Forrest, by Frank Crowley (2000); Australia's Western Third, by F.K. Crowley (1960); A New History of Western Australia, C.T. Stannage, Editor (1981); Aborigines of The West; Their Past and Their Present, R.M. and C.H. Berndt, Editors (1979); A Story Of A Hundred Years, Sir Hal Colebatch, Editor (1929); The Life of Herbert Hoover, by George H. Nash (1983); Maitland Brown: A View of Nineteenth Century Western Australia, by Peter Cowan (1988); Signor Pietro G. Porcelli, by Simon Keane (1982); Thomas Hill Dixon: First Superintendent of Convicts in Western Australia, by Tony Stebbing; Early Days Journal of the Royal Western Australian Historical Society (Inc) Vol 11, Part 5 (1999); A History of The Commissariat, Fremantle 1851-1991, by Ian Crawford, Anne Delroy, Lynne Stevenson (1992); Fremantle's Secret Fleets, by Lynne Cairns (1995); The Merchant Princes of Fremantle: The Rise and Decline of a Colonial Elite, by Patricia M. Brown (1996); A Place Of Consequence: A Pictorial History of Fremantle, by R. Reece and R. Pascoe (1983); An Incident At Fremantle, by B.K. De Garis, Labor History, No. 10 (1966); History of Timber Bridges in Western Australia, by P.M. Palmer, Western Roads (1979); A Basilica In The Making: The Centenary of St. Patrick's Fremantle, by Geraldine Byrne (2000); Hi Jinks At The Hot Pool: Mirror Reflects The Life of a City, by Ron Davidson (1994); The Footballers: A History of Football in Western Australia, by Geoff Christian, Jack Lee, Bob Messenger, Ray Jordan, Editor (1985); Football in WA Before 1900: A Fremantle Perspective, by Clement McIntryre (1979); No Fixed Address: The hunt for Brenden James Abbott, by Derek Pedley (1999).

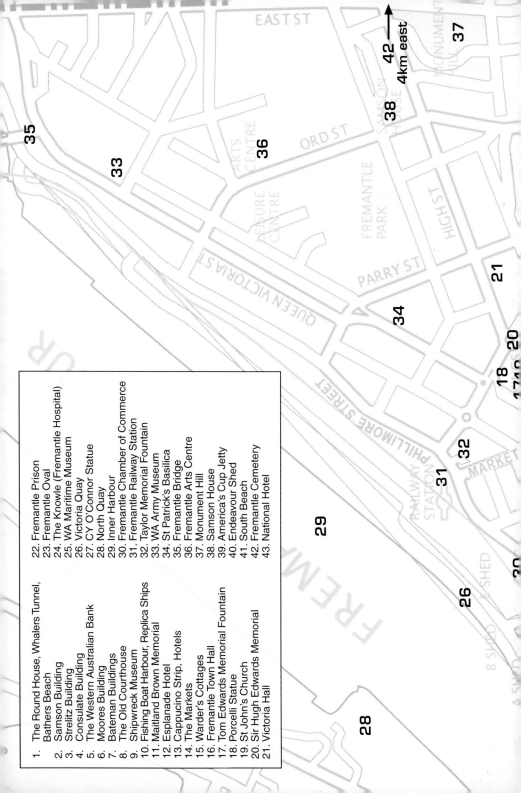

EAST ST

42
4km east

37

MONUMENT HILL

38

SAMSON HOUSE

ORD ST

35

33

36

ARTS CENTRE

LEISURE CENTRE

FREMANTLE PARK

HIGH ST

QUEEN VICTORIA ST

PARRY ST

21

34

18 20
17 19

32

PHILLIMORE STREET

31

MARKET

RAILWAY STATION

29

26

28

FREM

B SHED    D SHED

30

1.  The Round House, Whalers Tunnel,
    Bathers Beach
2.  Samson Building
3.  Strelitz Building
4.  Consulate Building
5.  The Western Australian Bank
6.  Moores Building
7.  Bateman Buildings
8.  The Old Courthouse
9.  Shipwreck Museum
10. Fishing Boat Harbour, Replica Ships
11. Maitland Brown Memorial
12. Esplanade Hotel
13. Cappucino Strip, Hotels
14. The Markets
15. Warder's Cottages
16. Fremantle Town Hall
17. Tom Edwards Memorial Fountain
18. Porcelli Statue
19. St John's Church
20. Sir Hugh Edwards Memorial
21. Victoria Hall

22. Fremantle Prison
23. Fremantle Oval
24. The Knowle (Fremantle Hospital)
25. WA Maritime Museum
26. Victoria Quay
27. CY O'Connor Statue
28. North Quay
29. Inner Harbour
30. Fremantle Chamber of Commerce
31. Fremantle Railway Station
32. Taylor Memorial Fountain
33. WA Army Museum
34. St Patrick's Basilica
35. Fremantle Bridge
36. Fremantle Arts Centre
37. Monument Hill
38. Samson House
39. America's Cup Jetty
40. Endeavour Shed
41. South Beach
42. Fremantle Cemetery
43. National Hotel